RADICAL
SELF
BELIEF

#ADULTING THE RALLY OF LIFE

THE ESSENTIAL ROADMAP FOR
SUSTAINABLE SUCCESS

Edition 2

THE QUANTUM DECISION MAKING PROGRAM™ SERIES

The Mojo Maker© Nikki Fogden-Moore

ALSO BY NIKKI

THE WAKE UP WORKOUT©

VITALITY
—Fresh Air, Fresh Food
and a Fresh Perspective

FITPRENEUR
—The Ultimate Leader, Healthy,
Wealthy and Wise

PRAISE FOR THE #ADULTING THE RALLY OF LIFE ROADMAP

I've always prided myself on having a positive attitude and always finding a solution when the chips were down. Then I just found I couldn't get myself out of the darkest spot—nothing was working, work wasn't working, family was something I was avoiding and I couldn't seem to make any clear decisions. Nikki's roadmap, checkpoints and step-by-step approach gave me an incredible re-route. A lighthouse in the storm—and I never stop using these tools now—they have shifted my perspective and my results. If you can't coach with Nikki, this book will be the next best thing!

M HOFFMAN
Founder and CEO, London

I have worked with Nikki for the past two years and I would have to say I have never felt more supported or believed in by anyone. My journey with Nikki has been an evolution, from a more tactical operational plan to get back in the driver's seat and integrate life fully the way I want, to a very spiritual, intuition-based, decision-making framework. Nikki has challenged me to continually let go and create space, which has been a big lesson for an A-type, always-on personality. The realisation that things are meant to be when they are in true alignment and happen with ease and grace rather than brute force has been life-altering for me. I truly feel that I am in the driver's seat. I feel grounded and more connected to my higher self and my purpose than ever before. Thanks, Nikki, for your belief and unwavering support and commitment.

ALEXIE OB
Advisory Board, COO, Melbourne

There is no going back once you start working with Nikki.
*We thought we were pretty self-aware but she helped us unpack the
stories we told ourselves that were holding us back, helped us uncover
what we really want and realise that we deserve to have all that and
more. Working as a couple with Nikki has been a seamless way of
enriching our life journeys together. We are now operating from our
true selves, with more confidence, creativity and heart than we ever
thought possible. Our children, our families, our relationship and our
businesses and community have all benefited from our growth. It's
been confronting but Nikki has been our champion, guiding us through
with complete honesty, love and support! This book will be the ideal
navigator for you. It works.*

PAUL & DENIKER S
Media, Managing Director/Chairman Tasmania

Pick this book up, do the work and you'll never look back.
*The confronting thing is you may feel like everything you thought was
the right way to approach your life beforehand, you may turn that
around completely. That's where this is so awesome. I was challenged,
encouraged and empowered. Nikki knows her stuff—she deeply cares
and is the deliverer of the ultimate truth carrier. Be ready.*

SCOTT M
Partner in Law, New Zealand

*If you love the adrenaline in life and yet have lost your mojo, this book will
get it back for you, and then some! I already sold my business and was
in the middle of the next adventure when it all went downhill. I learned
to embrace all my experience and have a totally new sense of purpose—
getting to know my 'ego' was a huge step and has been a game changer.
Nikki will get you to the podium, then ensure you stay there!*

CHRIS S
CEO, San Francisco

FOR TRUE LEADERS IN LIFE YOU ARE THE PIONEER YOU PAVE THE WAY BE BRAVE BE AUTHENTIC BE ON PURPOSE "

-Nikki

COPYRIGHT

PREFACE

There are moments in life that are truly defining. When I first wrote this book I called it *#Adulting The Rally of Life,* as it is an analogy I use so often in working with my clients. Navigating all the ups and downs, highs and lows we go through—seeing the world with a different lens. Embracing it all.

The expression is crucial to me, as my role is to ensure I get people back in the driver's seat. Instead of the backseat, on autopilot and handing their power over to others, the system to fear, shame, blame of feeling disempowered and overwhelmed.

To truly shift from chaos to calm for sustainable success. Whatever that may look like to you—it is about knowing, trusting and having faith in the NOW as much as the future.

As I write this preface I'm with my my parents in NZ and my father is navigating a difficult time at 91. I had some time to reflect. To chat with some clients about practicing what we preach.

That the advice in this book was a set of proven tools I deploy myself, especially in times of high mental and emotional demand. That writing each chapter, and designing each model is based on raw experience in my own world and the way I work with the incredible people I coach and mentor.

To me this book is about truly unlocking the best self sufficiency we have—radical self belief. Making it a "doing book" for real life.

I asked myself: What do you (the Reader) get when you use this book as I have intended it?

- What do you get when you have real awareness?
- What do you get when you are consistently accountable?
- What do you get when you consciously take action in your life—one step at a time?

You get Radical Self Belief.

The ability to know yourself, to plan with resonance, to observe with humility and to show up for yourself and for others authentically, no matter what is going on around you.

Remember—it's what we do, not what we say that matters. We need to know we are enough, we do have the skills and the ability to find support and adjust direction as often as required. We are significant, our vision for life (whatever it may be) has meaning and purpose. We need to redirect the coordinates away from fear, towards curiosity. Away from blame and shame, towards ownership and accountability. Away from external validation, towards an internal GPS that lights the way in the darkest of times.

That is radical self belief.

Dear Reader—please enjoy this book. Apply the tools. Ask yourself the questions. You are the master of your destiny. You are in the driver's seat.

And lastly, this book is also for you Trevor. I will carry your legacy, your strength, your tenacity and your will in all I do. Your daughter, forever connected.

Nikki
June 2021

ACKNOWLEDGEMENTS

To anyone who has the courage to do things with life, this book is for you.

To all of the clients I have worked with over the past twenty-plus years, this is in memory of the moments when it really felt like your world was caving in, the midnight SOS calls came or we shared our deeper strategy days. To the teams, the founders and CEOs who are courageous enough to work with me—as you know, I get straight to the point. I seek the truth and a path less travelled, because I know there is another way of operating that ensures we thrive instead of striving all the time.

To each of you, thank you for all you have taught me in return and the journeys we have taken together. This is for you.

Special thanks to my folks, who taught me so much about nature, loving life and gave me a level of awareness that has kept my face towards the sun. You gave me a life of fierce independence and taught me to be strong from within but to always be a light in this world.

I also want to mention the men and women on the Hawaii US Marine Corps Base, who welcomed me to their world for an unforgettable day on base a few years back. Training and talking with different battalions and specialist divisions has left such an impact on me. Your personal stories have stayed with me all this time, and to some extent, this book reflects much of the philosophy around extreme accountability and living by choice, not chance. It reflects being on purpose and the vital art of regrouping. Many of the conversations we had about agility and faith inspired me as I wrote this book.

To James Hunter, Al Ramadan and to 'Gayle', your voices were in my head as I finished this. Thank you.

We are so lucky to live in a world where anything is possible if you put your mind to it—the trick is to learn to unlock that thinking and lean into the corners. That's where all the magic happens.

Welcome to the journey.

Nikki

CONTENTS

"

The truth is that while most adults physically "grow up," they never quite reach emotional or psychological adulthood. In other words, most "grown-ups" aren't really adults at all. This leaves most people in a state of puerile fears, angers and traumas that fester away in the unconscious mind for decades.[1]

"

---

1   Alethia Luna Loner Wolf/Inner Child Work.

    RADICAL SELF BELIEF

adulting

/ˈadʌltɪŋ,əˈdʌltɪŋ/

noun; informal

the practice of behaving in a way characteristic
of a responsible adult, especially the accomplishment
of mundane but necessary tasks[2]

---

2   Oxford Dictionary.

"LEAN IN"

FOREWORD

Your life is becoming more complex and confusing—isn't it!

Our work and life priorities are inextricably defined by devices and our inbox, while face-to-face communication and collaboration are skills we teach graduates upon joining the workplace.

Our work, community and society are increasingly digitised, mechanised, and despite the prevalence of the Internet and social media, many of our employees feel more disconnected than ever before.

Our mental illness epidemic is becoming worse—one in five Australians* aged sixteen to eighty-five experience a mental illness in any given year. The most common mental illnesses are depression, severe anxiety and substance use disorder, often occurring in combination. Thirty people attempt suicide daily; six die.[3]

Our shareholders seek greater profitability, with efficiency sought by greater work, augmented through artificial intelligence, robotic-process automation, and a data and analytical world driven by ubiquitous 'Internet of things'. Meanwhile, our roles for which we have been trained for decades become marginalised or redundant.

---

3   *[Black Dog Institute Research 2019].

As leaders, we are increasingly being encouraged to disrupt, differentiate and innovate our workplaces, our teams and our organisations—and to adopt 'agile workplaces' with limited consideration of the impacts on friendships, social networks in the workplace and our organisation's 'soul and heart'.

What follows is complex and confusing. It is also overwhelming.

The answer is chaos.

How will you adapt and succeed in this chaotic world? It isn't fiction; we are living in this world today.

In *Radical Self Belief #Adulting The Rally of Life,* Nikki Fogden-Moore brings to life twenty years of research and case studies of people like you working across various sectors. Nikki is the Mojo Maker. She examines how to assess and regain your mojo and your courage and confidence to be in control of your life's directions and decisions, as well as how to define your priorities.

To regain control, who better than Nikki to guide us in this chaotic world?

When I first met Nikki, I was immediately struck by her intellect, insight and EQ—a powerful trifecta! Nikki had an uncanny ability to ask incisive questions to deeply understand me: what really drives me, my views on issues, how I operate in work and life, and how I make decisions. And then there was Nikki's authenticity, a real integrity and openness, and with it a vulnerability which provoked a reciprocity of truths. Nikki's ideas are not theory; her comments and observations are based on personal experiences, those she discusses with so many amazing people and senior leaders globally. This authenticity and depth of insight makes *#Adulting* a truly unique book.

Nikki shared her plans for this book when we completed the Leadership Podcast. It is a book initiated through so many CEOs and leaders sharing their interest in a pragmatic and easy-to-read guide to operating in a world tilting towards chaotic.

If you are expecting a book that merely validates how you currently operate, you will be disappointed—but hopefully also surprised.

The #Adulting roadmap will challenge you. It will change your perspectives and force you to rethink how you operate at home, with family and friends, and in so many situations at work. It will force you to consider who is in your 'pit crew' and whether you surround yourself with people who truly want you to be successful.

Life isn't linear, and for all your 'best-intentioned plans', it rarely follows a predetermined path. It is how you respond to life's deviations, challenges and the unexpected, sometimes traumatic events that will be crucial to your long-term success. And in a world Nikki terms 'Generation Exhibition', it is your direction, decisions and success that matter, not what others think.

Making your values-based decisions takes courage, self-confidence and a moral compass you possess and need to leverage.

I would encourage everyone in a leadership position grappling with these challenges to read *#Adulting The Rally of Life— The Essential Roadmap For Sustainable Success,* so you can understand the path from chaos to calm and regain your confidence to truly achieve your full potential.

James Hunter
National Managing Partner, KPMG

"STARTLINE WHERE THE RUBBER HITS THE ROAD"

overwhelm

/əʊvəˈwɛlm/

verb

bury or drown beneath a huge mass of something

synonyms: swamp, submerge, engulf, bury,
deluge, flood, inundate, clog, saturate, glut, overload,
beset, overburden, snow under

THE VITAL STATISTICS
OVERWHELM

JC

46% OF STAFF LEAVE DUE TO BURN OUT

46%

46% of respondents blame burnout for up to half of their staff quitting each year. Kronos and Future Workplace Survey 2019.

US$300 BILLION IS SPENT ON BURN OUT & OVERWHELM

$300B

Burnout is estimated to cost the US economy alone $300 billion annually according to a recent article by Workplace Psychology

83% OF US WORKERS SUFFER STRESS

83%

83% of US workers suffer from work-related stress. Everest College Study 2019.

US$77 BILLION COSTS DUE TO DEPRESSION

$77B

Depression leads to $51 billion in costs due to absenteeism and $26 billion in treatment costs.

THE MOJO MAKER™

RADICAL SELF BELIEF

" A NEW TERRAIN REQUIRES A NEW ROADMAP "

-Nikki

WELCOME

In today's modern world of accessibility and digital revolution, the epidemic of overwhelm and its effect on society has reached an all-time high. The speed at which we live our lives, work, handle information, create transactions and interact with multiple people at any one time is both exhilarating and overwhelming. AI, UI, EI, robotics, automation, blockchain—the list goes on.

As technological advances have given rise to globalisation and opened the world up for trade in the last forty to fifty years, competition has become fierce and the corporate landscape has changed dramatically. The landscape we operate in today is like nothing we've experienced before.

In this New Age of Self Reliance,[4] we may have unwittingly removed any sense of self. In essence, we are running our lives in a modern world with a very outdated internal set of decision-making frameworks.

The more connected we become online and with automation, the more fragmented and disconnected we become in our interpersonal relationships and, more importantly, from the perspective of and relationship we have with ourselves. This increased speed of business, social media pressure, and lack

---

4   Harvard Business Review.

of time for self, family and friends are leaving people feeling helpless, hopeless, disconnected and exhausted.

> *In essence, our internal programming has not undergone the updates everything else around us has.*

We need to get back to basics and reset the place from which we make our decisions. There is a need for a simple approach. We are losing our sense of self, trust and navigation. Many people are in survival mode, using an old road map and an outdated operating system for a completely new landscape.

OVERWHELM IS AN EPIDEMIC

In 2019, overwhelm created a 300-billion-dollar industry[5] in the US alone, yet it's not getting better.

Lack of focus, overwhelm and opting out constitute a global epidemic affecting all ages. Teenagers and children as young as four and five are already displaying attributes of overwhelm, anxiety and depression.

---

5   Workplace Psychology.

Recent research shows that overwhelm has increased tenfold in the last thirty years.[6] Paradoxically, we have more wellbeing services, mindfulness sources and resources, and HR and mental-health plans in place than ever before.

As Stephen Hawking said, we have entered 'the century of complexity'.

Despite the billions of dollars spent on HR, corporate psychology and other programs and resources, we are still missing a fundamental piece of the puzzle: There is too much advice focusing on what is wrong and not enough focusing on a fast track to recovery or preventing problems in the first place.

Kronos and Future Workplace[7] surveyed 614 US human resources professionals at organisations with 100 to over 2,500 employees. The result: 46% of respondents blame burnout for up to half of their staff quitting each year.

So many of our leaders are running at a pace that far outweighs the perks and processes in place to grow organically and with sustainable success. The pressure to perform is hitting multiple generations, some with little or no experience at all, as we have a new paradigm in place.

Entrepreneurial growth gives way to waves of new generations all climbing their way to the top job, latest hot start-up or Internet sensation.

---

6   Workplace Psychology.
7   https://www.kronos.com/about-us/newsroom/employee-burnout-crisis-study-reveals-big-workplace-challenge-2017

RADICAL SELF BELIEF

Unlike three decades ago, where a few big companies generated most of the jobs in each country, it is entrepreneurs who generate most of the jobs in today's world. Our jobs are created by an emerging talent of founders, start-up-focused leaders, budding small-business owners and pioneers who have built their own businesses from scratch, whether it's a small coffee shop, an insurance business or one of the latest takeaway-food franchise companies to burst onto the scene.

THE PRESSURE TO SUCCEED

This pressure to lead and succeed, define and design a life you love straight out of university or school has catapulted our industrial revolution into a revolution of individual leaders. The fact that the drive to succeed and be 'someone' is the focus of our children's education from the start, regardless of age or gender, points to a world where it is never enough.

Leaders as young as twenty-one are handling the turnover and operational decision-making that comes with rapid growth. Persistent demands from diverse stakeholders to improve performance impose substantial stressors on CEOs. Frequent, intense and unpredictable interactions with elements of the task environment potentially increase CEOs' emotional exhaustion and depersonalisation from the strategic process.

On top of this, workplace culture has changed dramatically and personal relationships have taken a back seat, with many employees staying in a job for less than three years due to burnout and a sense of disconnection and discontentment.

We are experiencing the highest levels in history of burnout, exhaustion and depression, whether that be in our leadership, in our schools, in our universities or in our workplaces. Employee burnout (which leads to overwhelm) is cited as a psychological response to chronic work stress resulting from a combination of emotional exhaustion, depersonalisation, reduced personal accomplishment and reduced professional efficacy.[8]

Burnout has many contributing factors that build up over time. According to the World Health Organisation (WHO) and their recent studies around workplace stress and overwhelm, our ability to handle stress and to spiral into survival mode can be categorised into two areas:
- contents
- context

We can equally apply these classifications to classrooms, homes and other areas of life and work.

For example, one could ask the following:
- What are the contents of our life/day/study time/work and what is the context in which we operate or feel is significant as a part of that landscape?
- Is our workload too high? Is our study monotonous? Are we excluded from decision-making at home or at work?

Furthermore, in what context do we experience these issues? Is there a lack of career development and promotion opportunities? Are interpersonal relationships at work creating tension? So, we lack support in the home environment?[9]

---

8   (Cordes and Dougherty, 1993; Halbesleben, 2006; Jackson et al., 1986).
9   World Health Organization Workplace Stress 2019 https://www.who.int/ occupational_health/topics/stressatwp/en/

Panic, fear and isolation have a ripple effect.

Burnout is an effect of overwhelm. Overwhelm is a serious issue. We can't keep treating the symptoms; we need to find the source. It's time we looked up at the horizon ahead of us and became personally accountable for the cornerstones in our lives, both professionally and personally.

This does not involve the usual programming of punching through challenges and life only to be exhausted, deflated and burnt out. Instead, it requires the other perspective: the curiosity to take the road less travelled, in turn discovering why it will be your most rewarding journey.

THE ROAD OUT OF OVERWHELM

I believe we have a cure for overwhelm. I believe that 'cured' or engaged leaders, founders, CEOs and entrepreneurs can rebuild their business and personal lives for the benefit of their shareholders, employees, family and customers—and themselves.

I have witnessed so many people work hard, push through and fight with all of their might to get to where they are today only to feel beaten down and exhausted. They carry 'wins' that, in the scheme of things, are all too fleeting, and they have experienced serious collateral damage along the way.

We can change technology, but we are not evolving our internal human hard drive and decision-making frameworks (values/ expectations) at the same speed.

Albert Einstein famously said that doing the same thing over and over again and expecting different results is the definition of insanity.

So, we can't keep doing the same thing in our personal and professional lives and expect a different outcome. We need to change how we approach all things with a fresh perspective.

Instead of a white-knuckled ride, where we have a sense of impending doom lurking around every corner and we breathe a sigh of relief when we finally get some good news, what about a thrill-seeking, energised, all-in flow of being in the driver's seat?

Accordingly, we might consider the following:

What if overwhelm and burnout statistics dramatically reduced because we actually empowered our leaders with the fundamental mindset of mastering the rally of life?

What if we didn't focus so much on the symptoms and building platforms to 'catch the fall-out and manage the disease of complexity' but, rather, we educated each individual leader? What if we educated them on the innate multi-dimensional gifts we all possess to have vision, mission and purpose and learn to trust an inner GPS—one far greater than society's outdated expectations?

IT'S PERSONAL

The race of life may stay the same over centuries, but it's how we handle the landscape that needs to be different. It is a full stepping up for personal ownership and integrity. This book is

the toolbox, the roadmap, the navigator for empowering you to do just that.

Companies, communities, families and individuals are all facing the same issues. We can't keep focusing on external tools and resources and expect a quick fix—we must go within and adjust our perspective, our approach and our capacity for life. The solution to overwhelm is instilling inner confidence, wisdom, the ability to work well with others and co-create.

With this book I am determined to be a part of the change. I am determined to provide a new kind of 'roadmap' to navigate the rally of today's modern world, one that empowers individuals to be aware, take action and be accountable.

That is what Radical Self Belief #Adulting The Rally of Life is designed to do. It will

- empower you to identify where you are at any given stage, get out of survival mode, recognise the signs of overwhelm, understand the difference between self-talk (ego) and self (our inner GPS or intuition);
- help to declutter the confusion to assess all relevant resources, tools, science and revelations and put them into practice without turning everything upside down and without causing further overwhelm;
- harness the unique and most valuable commodity of all—that human sense of unconditional love, connectivity, contribution and significance in all we do; and
- identify the goals that you REALLY want and build your resources, people and trajectory to get there.

ON A MISSION

The ability to evolve is true strength and an asset for all of us as we move forward in our lives as leaders. Over the past twenty years, I have had the privilege of working side by side with some of the most incredible people, people with visionary minds and hearts. I have worked with founders and executives, managers and CEOs, athletes, artists and entrepreneurs.

Whether it's navigating a global advertising career, managing individuals through their leadership journey, or running Boardroom Retreats™, I am in the trenches with my clients and have been working in this space, coaching high-performance individuals and organisations for thousands of hours and in places across the world.

Committed to growth and the ability to define, design, be agile and work with others in true co-creation and collaboration. Teamwork makes dreams work.

> *This Mission is underpinned by my uber focused dedication ensure that the majority of the world's wealth is managed and grown by the next generation of value-led leaders with the highest integrity, drive and courage.*

- That we may have an abundance of good money, ideas, vision and purpose flowing across this globe; and
- That our companies are grown, handled, invested in and passed on by people who are accountable, passionate, visionary and kind.

YOU ARE IN THE DRIVER'S SEAT

You need to be number one in your life as you lead; to invest in yourself; and to 'adult' and make decisions for the highest good for yourself and others. As a leader, this is a valuable tool. Why?

You are at the forefront. You are the pioneer. You are leading by example. Stop looking around; you're it.

This connection with self is vital to embrace life with all it has to offer; to lead with truth, transparency and transformation of how we lead within ourselves and how we show up for others.

If we want the next generation to thrive, we have to start doing things differently. We have to ensure our engines are tuned and each of us as individuals are up to the task in our own way.

Using the old paradigm for measuring success and pushing through life is *like putting a lawn mower engine into a Formula 1 car.* It won't perform the same, no matter how good the technology is that surrounds it.

There is an easier way of doing things. It is time to replace the need to constantly 'overachieve and strive' with a set of tools that will help you enjoy the journey and thrive, whatever is thrown your way. In this book, I am going to demonstrate how to actually do that—how to suit up, show up and be significant, without the need for anyone else's validation.

Now more than ever, we have access to tools and information around awareness, dismantling beliefs that no longer serve us. Reframing our mindset, meditation, the art of being present, and the human brain's ability to re-program and reshape itself through neuroplasticity. How do we discern the steps that will take us from chaos to calm and help us feel more in control? This can be achieved by:

- working on the individual and their sovereign self (personal accountability);
- creating a new framework (roadmap) for decision-making and a perspective about life that embraces uncertainty instead of fearing it;
- having a clear framework for decision-making; and
- a roadmap where leaders can rebuild their businesses and personal lives for the benefit of their shareholders, employees, customers, family and, most importantly, for themselves.

That is *Radical Self Belief #Adulting The Rally of Life.* The book is for leaders in life and organisations so they can return to the driver's seat and gain back 'control'.

rally
ral.ly 1 (răl′ē)

verb
ral·lied, ral·ly·ing, ral·lies

v.tr.
1. to call together for a common purpose; assemble
2. to reassemble and restore to order
3. to rouse or revive from inactivity or decline

v.intr.
1. to come together for a common purpose
2. to join in an effort for a common cause
3. to recover abruptly from a setback

"MY MANTRA: DO NOT BUILD TOWERS ON QUICKSAND; SUSTAINABLE CREATIONS ARE ON A SOLID FOUNDATION."

—Nikki

HOW TO USE THIS BOOK

Life is like a rally—all conditions, all seasons, all terrains. No one comes and sweeps the rubble off the road for you.

This isn't your first rodeo. Or mine. I am committed to working with the world's very best value-driven leaders to put them firmly in the driver's seat.

We have two choices: wing our way through it, or live our life with purpose.

To be on the podium you need a strong sense of direction, an incredible pit crew, the right vital ingredients, a well-maintained engine, a compass and a sense of spirit.

This is my purpose. So, this really matters. You matter. It's not what happens to us; it's how we approach the race that really matters. It's time for a fresh perspective, to approach leading your life with a new frame of mind.

To do this, you must take the time to lay solid foundations, accept support and help where you need it. Consider what your true values and purpose are so you can be the successful CEO of your business and your life. You must be excited, prepared, on purpose and able to adjust coordinates when change is presented.

It's not about throwing everything away. It's about understanding the fact that life is organic and you get to choose what you will leave behind and what you will carry with you on each step of the journey.

This, however, is not a quick fix. It requires a fundamental change in viewpoint. Will you be the Passenger or the Pilot? Back seat or driver's seat?

In the coming pages, the tools and tips will empower you to swap the old 'strive/passenger' mentality for the 'thrive/driver's seat' mentality.

Strive:
- Giving 100%, pushing through with 'hard work', determination, dogmatic resilience, perseverance, and doing the same thing over and over again but expecting different results.
- Finding yourself repeatedly stuck in quicksand, tired and overwhelmed, experiencing highs and lows and peaks and troughs? Are fleeting wins quickly being replaced by another setback?

Versus

Thrive:
- Recognising that the landscape of life is all conditions and all seasons, and the best way to approach it is to change your perspective from passenger seat to driver's seat.
- To look at options, always know there is a solution and replace fear with curiosity.

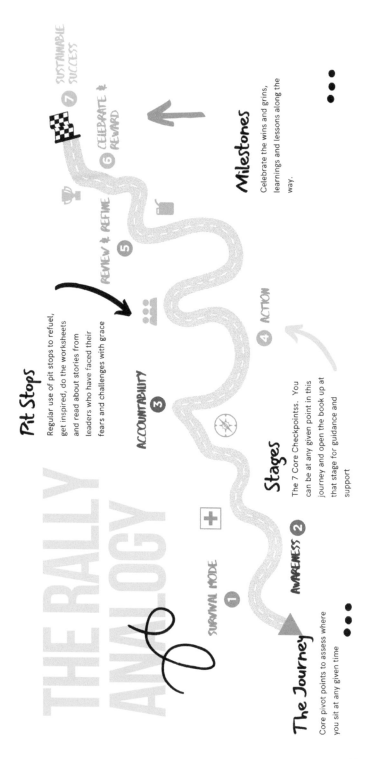

THE RALLY ANALOGY

Pit Stops

Regular use of pit stops to refuel, get inspired, do the worksheets and read about stories from leaders who have faced their fears and challenges with grace

Milestones

Celebrate the wins and grins, learnings and lessons along the way.

1. SURVIVAL MODE
2. AWARENESS
3. ACCOUNTABILITY
4. ACTION
5. REVIEW & REFINE
6. CELEBRATE & REWARD
7. SUSTAINABLE SUCCESS

Stages

The 7 Core Checkpointss. You can be at any given point in this journey and open the book up at that stage for guidance and support

The Journey

Core pivot points to assess where you sit at any given time

APPLYING THE RALLY ANALOGY

A heads-up that this book is written how I coach: candid, honest, raw and with real perspective. No hope projects. As I explained in the welcome, dreams do not work unless you do and great coaches work with you, not for you.

Each section is designed to give you the tools to go from chaos to calm at any given moment, on any given subject—no matter where you are in your life and leadership journey. They are designed to replace the chaos and uncertainty, the feeling of 'winging it', and the mentality of striving at all costs with being purpose-led, open-minded, enjoying the journey and thriving in any conditions.

Using the rally analogy, we navigate through each checkpoint and provide a sense of personal experience and foresight to feel supported, take stock of where you are now and identify where you need to go next.

A checkpoint can be linked to any given moment in your life, whether it's work or personal. It can also be applied to a project as a group.

1. **Checkpoint 1: Survival Mode**—What to do when you feel completely overwhelmed, can't go in any direction and are walking into the unknown.
2. **Checkpoint 2: Awareness**—Know where you are now and what really lights you up.
3. **Checkpoint 3: Accountability**—Understand your capabilities, who you need around you and what your vital ingredients are.
4. **Checkpoint 4: Action**—The steps needed to embark on your journey and how/what you need to do to get there.

5. **Checkpoint 5: Review and Refine**—Respect the conditions, press pause to review and refuel with regular pit stops.
6. **Checkpoint 6: Celebrate and Reward**—The wins and grins, podiums and teamwork ensure you embrace the journey, not just the destination.
7. **Checkpoint 7: Sustainable Success**—The ability to look ahead and anticipate while keeping your eyes on the road. Always be ready to take a new turn or be agile if one road closes.

It's not enough to just look at the map; you need to take the steps. At each stage I recommend you:
1. set clear expectations and outcomes,
2. do the pit stops and worksheets,
3. give yourself the allotted time,
4. utilise the tools and resources, and
5. go one checkpoint at a time.

SPEED

Go at your own pace.

This book is designed to assist you to take action in your world, not to push you through checkpoints at a pace with which you're not comfortable.

The seven checkpoints will bring together the models and proven tools and techniques that I use in the trenches coaching high-performing clients. These provide practical steps for you to go from chaos to calm and actually shift your perspective along the way, cementing one step before you move on to the next.

Note that sustainable success and moving from chaos to calm is more about agility than resilience. Yes, we need to be brave to learn and lean in and to bounce back; however, it is not about having to shoulder pain, guilt, shame and 'tough' moments and repeat that cycle to push through and exhaust yourself in the process, suppressing what you really want and 'soldiering on'— that is an outdated belief system.

Rather, this book will focus on agility, purpose, being present and having really good people around you.

SEE ME AS YOUR CO-DRIVER

A great coach or co-pilot does the journey with you, not for you. Throughout *Radical Self Belief #Adulting The Rally of Life* we will replace chaos, uncertainty, instability and autopilot with how to thrive in high performance. It's about focus, calm, agility, the awesome element of surprise, and who to delight in all the milestones.

We will replace a white-knuckled ride with a fully engaged excitement that you can handle and that allows you to thrive, be agile and navigate whatever comes your way. Focusing on these easy-to-use tools and tasks will help you clarify the core elements needed for each checkpoint.

Be open-minded so you can identify and acknowledge the roadblocks and the dangers, and then spend the majority of your time working on what you want—and not remaining stuck in the past or in the pain.

With that, you can regain clarity, connection and the confidence needed in life and business to trust your inner GPS. You can remain grounded no matter what is going on around you.
Then, we can fully embrace the journey.

KEEP IT SIMPLE

Ultimately, this is more than just understanding the roadmap; it is about actually using it. This means applying the tools to build a solid foundation you can pivot from rather than clinging to old frameworks that no longer support you on the journey.
In these pages, you will find a guidebook of sorts—a practical approach. The techniques in this book are very simple:

- be prepared to let go of old limiting beliefs that no longer serve you;
- be prepared to let go of excuses and stories that are not for your highest good; and
- be prepared to spend at least fifteen minutes on each stage to invest in yourself and really consider the answers that lie on the path in front of you, waiting to be revealed.

Most importantly, this book will give you a framework for regular pit stops, show you the importance of having the right fuel, explain when to take alternative routes, and show you why it is vital to celebrate all layers of the journey.

The models work. They are based on proven results, over 10,000+ hours of coaching and many, many success stories. But don't just take my word for it. In the coming chapters, I will include case studies from clients and global influencers.

Read, apply, write on the pages, print out the worksheets, share and re-read at any moment you feel like you need to come back to base and regain a sense of awareness and accountability.

Whatever got you to this point should be recognised. I would like to gently remind you that in your life, no matter what happens externally, you are in charge of your thoughts, mindset and actions.

Athletes and race drivers draw support for their performance in all areas of life. They have a blend of physical, commercial and mental training. You can too. We all need the same development as, to some degree, we are all athletes.

Are you prepared to really show up for yourself? Regardless of whether you are running a multinational company, a family business, creating worthy change in your community, or leading yourself into newer heights as an individual, parent or partner on your own path to purpose?

It's time to reclaim that sense of inner confidence. Know thyself, build on your own authentic skills, then stand in your authenticity as you work with a team around you to navigate the road ahead.

If you have vision, energy, drive, tenacity, integrity and pure grit when it comes to leading a life you love, then this book is for you.

At times, you may feel alone, overwhelmed, exhausted or just plain worn out and burnt out. I urge you to not opt out. As you work your way through this book, I want you to remember the 10/90 rule. Spend more time looking forward than back.

It's not a Formula 1 track where someone comes in and picks lint off the road before you head off again. It's all conditions, all seasons and predictably unpredictable. But that's where the beauty lies.

Applying the principles outlined here does not simply mean acknowledging what we know we should be doing but also putting your ideas into action. I invite you to come and join me as your navigator as you suit up, step up, carefully select your pit crew, and define your own vital ingredients for sustainable success.

As you make your way through the chapters and checkpoints of *#ADULTING,* you will find the answers you need for a simple approach to decluttering, building confidence and reducing overwhelm in this complicated world.

You will move towards an understanding that change does not have to mean conflict, and that we can approach things in today's complex world with clarity, vision and confidence.

To lean into the unknown, step out of old programming and beliefs and redesign a framework to be agile and embrace the rally of life—for all seasons, all conditions, all terrains.

You are in charge of your destiny. I'm just your navigator.

Welcome to *Radical Self Belief #Adulting The Rally of Life.* Let's get started.

Nikki

"LOOKING UNDER THE HOOD"

1

CHECKPOINT
SURVIVAL MODE

BURN OUT, FREAK OUT, OPT OUT— RECOGNISING THE SIGNS OF OVERWHELM

survival

sur·viv·al (sərˈvaɪ vəl)

noun

1. the act or fact of surviving
2. a person or thing that survives or endures, especially an ancient custom, observance, belief, et cetera.

adjective

of or for use in surviving, especially under adverse or unusual circumstances: survival techniques

Welcome to Checkpoint 1. If you're reading (or perhaps listening) to this book, the chances are you are not in the jungle being chased by a fierce lion.

However, you may have experienced a real sense of fear or anxiety, a grip in your chest, exhaustion, overload or panic—perhaps triggered by something as simple as an email popping up on your screen. If you have, then these are definitely physical and mental warning signs you need to be listening to.

Unlike a visible injury, overwhelm symptoms are often pushed aside as leaders plough their way through each day, week and challenge without a sense of real direction or connection.

Fear, shame, blame and guilt get in the way and override curiosity and confidence. This is especially true when exhaustion, long hours, heavy responsibility and a sense of burden kick in.

We often run our lives and our days being so busy looking down that we forget to look up. We don't realise that tiny clicks in coordinates can create major shifts in outcomes and we may have lost our way. We don't notice that the landscape has changed, yet we could be looking at an old map or navigation system.

It is a bit like what happens when you don't update your Google Maps and the road you're looking for isn't listed. This is how overwhelm creeps in: you continue to drive on the same road without stopping to pause and consider if you're heading in the right direction.

When you start to feel the wheels come off and you can't regain a sense of calm or balance, or even get rid of the white noise and self-talk, it's imperative you stop and do a check-in.

It's time to look under the hood, to recognise the signs of overwhelm in all aspects of life and work.

In this chapter, we will cover the elements that contribute to survival mode and some frameworks that will help you identify where you sit now. We will address what to do to acknowledge and move from that place of confusion to feeling like there is light at the end of the tunnel. We will look at the following:

- How to recognise the signs of overwhelm.
- Oxygen mask first—How to apply personal first aid when you hit that point of chaos.
- The SOS—Overcoming fear and judgement to reach out for help.

Why are so many people in survival mode in the first place? We'd never let our phone batteries get this low, so why do we let our own energy hit the red zone so often?

Overwhelm has insidiously crept in and manifested itself over recent years with massive impact: loss of business, mental health problems, marriage breakdowns, health issues, disjointed families, layoffs at work, addictions, financial breakdowns, obesity, substance abuse, loss of legacy, isolation, values breakdown, increased depression and anxiety, increased reliance on medications, unmanageability and dysfunction.

There is a fine line between creative, visionary hard work, and burnout. Feeling overworked, misunderstood, isolated and

exhausted is something most leaders think they just have to put up with: 'This is the price you pay when you're at the top.' Survival mode has become the new normal.

Burnout (overwhelm and exhaustion) leads to freak out (fear and isolation), and then ultimately to opting out (inertia, lack of action, feeling stuck). We know so many people lately have been experiencing real frustration, triggers, even outbursts of anger or just internalised friction. This reflects a build-up of resentment, fear, feeling stuck and not having a voice.

There is a deeper impact of overwhelm.

We are experiencing this on a global level with the deeply serious events that are shaping history—from vaccines to violence; from rioting to marches of solidarity; from education issues to co-parenting, custody, divorce and depression.

UNDERSTANDING THE DEEPER IMPACT

01

PERSONAL

Relationship breakdowns, divorce

Illness, depression, heart attacks, anxiety and reduced overall wellbeing

Lack of financial acuity and planning resulting in poor decision making and increased unserviceable debt

Parenting and partnership issues, communication breakdowns, child anxiety and increases in behavioural issues and diagnosises.

02

PROFESSIONAL

Loss of staff retention

Mistakes at work, productivity breakdown

Miscommunication, bullying, icing out and failure to speak up/lead

Reduced attention to detail, loss of turnover, job satisfaction and client retention, increased sick leave, no shows.

Defensive leadership and management, lack of transparency, market confidence loss

03

FINANCIAL

Increased debts, financial burdens and breakdowns in planning in family, work and community environments

Increased expenditure on mental health, burn out, stress, anxiety and illness

Busy, overworked, detached, exhausted and stuck in a rut do not constitute how we were designed to be.

Many of you are feeling that your world is turning upside down and that you're in a real state of unrest, even if it's just your own small ecosystem. Uprising or awakening, you can call it what you will. There is a real feeling of being fed-up, pent-up, pushed down and that you can't seem to hold back anymore. These times require a new perspective.

Researchers have found that the way people feel about the stress in their lives is a far more powerful predictor of their general health than any other measure. High blood pressure, arthritis, obesity, anxiety and depression are all problems that strike both those who have very little free time and those who feel as though they do.[10]

Understanding your stress levels, your mental perspective and how you are looking at any given situation, person, place or challenge, as well as managing your energy levels in times of chaos, is core to moving from fighting our way through life to thriving. Chances are that if you're not willing to do the growth and lean in, it will happen anyway and be taken out of your hands.

---

10 Brigid Schulte.

> ## *So, you may as well be designing what you want; otherwise, you'll just keep getting what you're given*

We can't keep doing the same thing over and over again and expect different results. And, yes, whilst much of burnout and pressure is placed on us by society and change, we are the architects of this operating system, of the rules, the regulations and the imposed new speed of life. The real, undeniable truth is that no one but you can change how you feel and what is important and how we navigate our way through these modern times.

We can't want more and then not be prepared to show up for ourselves and be accountable for the decisions we make along the way. The very first decision is whether or not you want to be on autopilot in your life, or agile and in the driver's seat. If you choose the latter, then it's imperative you take inventory on what is really going on in your own world at this point in time.

Whatever got you to this point, just know there is always a solution, always a new horizon and that you absolutely, undoubtedly deserve the very best this world has to offer.

" YOU ARE YOUR GREATEST ASSET "

-Nikki

 RADICAL SELF BELIEF

RECOGNISING THE SIGNS OF OVERWHELM

When was the last time you checked your vitals? How do you know you're in Survival Mode?

The issue is not that we don't know overwhelm, burnout and exhaustion exist; the issue is that, despite this awareness, many of us fail to identify it before it is too late. Usually, this is driven by the fear of appearing less successful and in control than we would like to be.

We try to hide the real mayhem and cover this up with an even more frantic attempt to keep up appearances, while underneath the surface we are madly treading water to keep our head above water. We can't keep driving on a wobbly wheel or using a gear box that keeps slipping, so 'falling apart' and looking under the hood to pull the engine apart and see what needs repairing is essential.

The fact is, there is change. It starts first, however, from within.

How do you recognise you're getting pulled off course and need to realign before you go off the road altogether? Are you operating on such low energy and mental capacity that you don't have much room left for one more bump in the road?

It's important to keep an eye on your personal dashboard. There's no point putting great paintwork on a car with a burnt-out engine. If you're overwhelmed, the first step is to recognise it. We can then do something about getting you out of that quicksand and into a feeling of clarity around what to do next.

Whether this is the first time that you find yourself in a state of inertia and disconnected from your own personal and commercial happiness or in a repetitive cycle of peaks and troughs, we all have moments when we experience a total lack of motivation and feel so stuck that we can't see a way through it.

Overwhelm starts off harmless but very quickly leads to serious ramifications when the symptoms go unnoticed and are not addressed. This is perception versus reality. Ignoring the signposts can take you down a road you may not easily find your way back from. Overwhelm can often be described as the feeling of being completely lost, like driving on a winding road at night in the rain without a map or headlights. There are so many options, but you have no idea which way to turn.

- **Lost**—can't see clearly/don't know what to do/ indecision.
- **Lonely**—can't ask for help/no one understands/feeling isolated.
- **Lack of direction**—can't move/stuck/locked in a state of chaos, with no sense of direction or the ability to change the situation.

In the following table, I've listed some common symptoms, signs and situations to help you identify whether you are in overwhelm and survival mode or able to sit with calm and clarity.

Take a moment to circle or write down the signs and symptoms you feel best describe your current mental, physical and emotional state. Open up the dialogue with yourself—starting on the next page.

Where do you sit right now?

SURVIVAL MODE—OVERWHELM INDICATORS	DRIVER'S SEAT—HEALTHY INDICATORS
• Angry snappy, loss of patience towards others	• Calm, collected
• Bright lights, noises and busy places overwhelm and cause discomfort	• Choose your environments with ease
• Not really hearing well, foggy thinking and lack of energy	• Energised
• Emotionally shut down	• Connected and present
• Defensive	• Trusted
• Impatient	• Self-belief
• Adrenaline	• Believed in
• Anxious/Anxiety	• Engaged
• Unable to see the happy in anything for very long, if at all	• Focused
• Fear of loss, judgement, a gripping sensation that things are going wrong	• Quality experiences
• Overloaded	• Healthy mental and physical choices
• Stressed	• Clear-headed
• Exhausted	• Harmony in self and with others
• Burnt out	• Balanced energy levels
• Insomnia, trouble sleeping	• Healthy sleep patterns
• Craving sugar, alcohol, increased use of substances	• Good food choices
• Lonely, yet not alone	• Personal boundaries for time and space
• Disconnected/disengaged/ uninterested	• Connected to own ideas and trust
• Feeling like life is mundane and overly repetitive	• Creative, idea generation
• Depression	• Positive and balanced mental approach
• Extreme self-doubt	• Curious
• Avoiding decision-making, responsibility, planning, Financial loss, lack of day-to-day performance	• Happy and able to see the bright side of life
• Unmotivated	• Confident
• Isolated	• Motivated
• Inability to concentrate, need to numb out feelings and avoid sitting with self	• Inclusive
	• Non-reactive, secure in self
	• Easily spend time on projects and be with self without distraction
	• Truthful, clear, present and aware

Other observations:

_____

_____

_____

_____

_____

_____

_____

_____

_____

_____

RECOGNISING THE SIGNS OF OVERWHELM

 **Physical**

Exhaustion

Insomnia

Addictions (drugs, alcohol, sugar, etc)

Lack of energy

Weight gain/sudden weight loss

Muscle ache

Headaches

 **Mental**

Fuzzy or foggy thinking

Feeling 'stuck'

Anxiety

Inability to make decisions or focus

Fear of judgement from others

Over thinking

Procrastination

Rash or poor decisions

 **Emotional**

Emotionally shut down

Lack of connection to self or others

Feeling isolated and misunderstood

Argumentative

Defensive

Withdrawn

Avoidant

Depression/sadness/grief and guilt

OXYGEN MASK FIRST

Most people wait until they hit rock bottom or get pushed out of their comfort zone before they look at what was keeping them stuck in the first place.

Knowing you are in crisis mode is one step; taking the action to get help and move from chaos to calm is the vital next step. This is putting your own oxygen mask on first. As a leader in your life you need to be courageous. If you keep pushing through overwhelm and don't stop when you start to recognise the signs, it's like continuing to drive at full speed on a wonky wheel—it is only going to end in disaster.

Programs, coaching, counselling, and resources don't work unless we want to be helped and to change the way we do things from our own individual start line before anything else. It means being willing to recognise the signs and then take the next step to do something about it.

It means being able to identify when things are out of alignment and tackling any issues as they arise rather than burying them deep down only to have them resurface later with greater effect. It is crucial we all recognise as early as possible that true leadership means putting your oxygen mask on first.

How are you going to show up for yourself?

Our children and staff receive mentoring, coaching and continuing education. As a leader, a parent, a partner, why don't you? Even though we know what the right thing to do is, we can find ourselves completely unable to act or ask for help when we are faced with the idea of conflict or judgement.

Also, investing in yourself is not just for the times of chaos; it carries through as an evolution, growth and continuous learning. One of my clients (a founder and CEO) told me the other day that the CFO questioned why her leadership coaching was on their P&L and had said, 'Shouldn't you make that a personal expense and claim it back?' To which she answered, 'We invest in constant training and development for our staff, why should that not be the case for me—the one who created this business in the first place?'

You can handle anything. It's the view you take: Driver or backseat passenger? Past or present? Stuck or in motion?

- To step up, suit up and command a higher consciousness for your decision-making.
- To not remain stuck for fear of failure and the past, but to realise you are probably being triggered and pushed to break free of all that and pave your own way.
- To be accountable for putting on your own oxygen mask first.

To do this, go through and begin listening to your body and really paying attention to your anxiety levels, decision-making abilities and the feeling of being focused and calm. If you are in survival mode, the immediate action to take is:

1. Recognise the signs (as above).
2. Recalibrate in your own mindset that your wellbeing is a priority—so, have a look at the very first things you can do to stop overwhelm and take a breath. Take note: 'I can't be there for others unless I am well and clear-headed'.

3. Write down from the above signs where you feel you sit on the dashboard of stress and burnout and then identify the areas of your life that are causing the most stress and conflict—there is the Traffic Light Worksheet at the end of this checkpoint to guide you through this.

4. Once you have taken a moment to accept what this really is, then you have a chance to do something about it. You can create a tiny shift out of survival mode and into neutral until we can get your breath back and remove the cloud and confusion.

If you can relate to the majority of the population of leaders, parents and partners who look in the mirror and feel the greatest sense of anxiety and fear when they realise that they are stuck, the facade is coming off and there is nowhere left to go. They have reached the end of the road and are not sure where to go next.

- lost,
- lonely
- lack-lustre about life.

This is your chance to really create a shift. Please do not let shame, blame, fear, guilt or others limiting beliefs —the internal subconscious handbrakes—get in the way of you turning all of this around.

Pledge to show up for yourself. See the worksheet at the end of this checkpoint to note down your commitment to self. I also want to remind you here that part of this is being brave enough to ask for help and let people know you're in survival mode in the first place.

THE SOS—HOW TO REACH OUT TO OTHERS

Reaching out and getting support. One of our bigger afflictions as leaders is that we don't want to be vulnerable; via old programming, we may feel it will undermine our credibility and our value—and what we're 'selling', whether it's in a personal or commercial way.

This is part of first aid in survival mode: knowing you are not alone. I call it the SOS. Sharing the great times is one thing, but remarkable and sustainable success requires a different type of self-awareness and dedication to how we communicate when things are not going well.

What is stopping you from putting your hand up and registering the fact that you are not okay and the path you're currently on is not a very healthy one, neither mentally, emotionally or physically? It's time to do a quick pit stop so you can ponder some important questions before moving on:

- Are you investing in yourself?
- Are you paying attention to your own finances, wellbeing, happiness and vital ingredients, or just focused on everyone else?
- What is holding you back and keeping you stuck?
- What is your biggest fear if you were to reach out and let someone key to you know that you're not doing OK?
- Do you feel like you have failed and that vulnerability is a weakness?

Are you asking yourself, everything I have built is no longer viable, so does that mean I am no longer viable? Are you afraid of the judgement? Is asking for help in your position putting you on edge?

There is an innate difference between leaning into the corners and having curiosity around making mistakes, and fear of failure and conflict and avoiding these for so long that we get pushed to make a change whether we like it or not.

Realising that being vulnerable is in fact getting to know yourself better and that the only way to go from ground zero is up. It is understanding that this world we live in, with all its crazy chaos, means it's time to fully embrace the ever-changing landscape and replace fear with curiosity.

> "
> *Vulnerability will only become dangerous when it is not seen as an opportunity for growth and evolution, or when the signs of misalignment, disconnection and overload are ignored and suppressed.*
> "

Vulnerability can then put your health and your wellbeing at severe risk. If you turn it around and recognise that you have a choice to see your lessons in life as learnings, as new terrain, and that you can evolve through them, then you will be empowered to shift, to accelerate and to achieve more in life than you could ever imagine.

Don't let fear of other people's past reactions stop you from reaching out to build your better future and get yourself out of quicksand. By not doing this, by ignoring the signs, by pushing through and suppressing what is really going on, you avoid the possibility of change, support and calm. This will keep you trapped longer in the feeling of overwhelm, and this can have dire consequences.

The greatest action we can make once we acknowledge that something is not quite right is to have the courage to put our hand up, speak up and actually let someone else know we are not okay. Letting people know you're not okay, is okay. In fact, it is a vital part of adulting the rally of life. It shows self-worth and value. So hard, I know, particularly if you have not honoured that feeling before.

This very acknowledgement creates a foundation whereby you have finally accepted that you matter.

Reaching out is like sending up a flare, or dropping a last known GPS point on a road map to ensure others know where you are when there is a storm.

Here are some basic pillars to set in place.

1. Seek Out the Right Support
Whatever the time or circumstance, there needs to be someone you can reach out to first.

Choose someone you trust, regardless of their relationship to you—the ability to be open is the most important factor. If you do not know anyone directly, then I always say reach out to a

professional organisation. You may have one in your workplace, or you could reach out to one of the many reputable and established organisations and foundations that exist to be the first line of response when you feel completely stuck.

Examples of people you may trust include a spouse, mentor, trusted colleague or best friend. Professional organisations include the HR department at your company, Beyond Blue, Outside the Locker Room, the Red Cross, your doctor, counsellor, coach or professional advisor.

2. Speak Up

Just say the first few words—all you need to do is put your hand up. "I am not OK" is usually enough at the moment, because if you are sharing this with the right person, they will instantly know. In Checkpoint 3 - Accountability, I take you through the truth matrix and how to have conflict-free conversation. For now, however, for the very first step, keeping it simple is all you need to do.

Trained professionals and people who know you well will understand that just acknowledging you have a problem took enormous courage. If you're doing this in a personal setting, then a very simple one- or two-sentence dialogue is all you need.

Note that when you are sharing this information in survival mode, you can feel nausea, anxiety, extreme stress, exhaustion and the real reaction of fear. This is normal, as you are moving out of your comfort zone completely. So, be patient and kind to yourself, and know you are supported by just the very fact that you are showing up to share and acknowledge that things are not okay.

Here are some helpful scripts to use as a framework:

'I want to share something in complete trust and confidence.'

'I don't feel like explaining it all right now; I'm just trying to put my hand up and say "Hey, I'm probably not doing great".'

'I feel... (insert how you actually feel).'

'I am afraid that by sharing this with you I will seem weak/ vulnerable/silly, and right now I couldn't handle a negative reaction to trusting you with something extremely important to me.'

'Please be patient, as just acknowledging this is hard.'

'I'd appreciate you being able to acknowledge that this is in the strictest of confidence.'

'Thank you for listening without needing to solve this right now.'

Take your script with you—don't ad-lib the conversation. Know also that it's like learning to ride a bicycle with training wheels. You may not get it right first up; you might get speed wobbles and you might feel sick. It can literally cause a physical reaction when we have to share our truths or most vulnerable moments with others.

Listening is a skill.

If someone is coming to you with this information, please make the time to listen to them. It takes great courage to put your hand up and admit when you're in overwhelm and survival mode.

If you're hearing this from someone (so you're the listener), please create a safe place and don't ask too many questions upfront. It's hard enough just to acknowledge that there is a problem—when someone is overwhelmed, pushing them to explain how they feel or why they feel that way can be far too much. A good example of the bare, basic conversation could be as follows:

Person A: *I have to let you know I'm not doing okay; I feel overwhelmed and it took a lot of courage for me to come to you to share this.*

Person B: *Thank you for trusting me with this information. I hear you and see you. Would it be okay for me to ask some questions and see how we can best go from here? (If they say no, I would create a pause to ensure they have time to just sit safely on the phone or in front of you, and then perhaps ask if you can advise, for example, a manager/professional).*

STEPS TO LISTEN AND ACKNOWLEDGE

As a listener/receiver, here are three vital steps you can take when someone chooses to confide in you.

1. Acknowledge (I see you):
'Thank you for trusting me with this— you have my word that this is in confidence.'

2. Ask (I hear you):
'What is one thing you need to feel safe and secure now that you have shared this information with me?'

3. Align (you matter):

'Can I have your permission to let (insert manager, HR director, board member, significant other, coach, teacher, et cetera) know that you are not doing okay, so that we can confidently make a next step together? If not, I would like to be able to follow up tomorrow and see what we can do next.'

If you feel that anyone sharing this critical information with you is in danger and you are unsure what to do next, call a helpline from one of the organisations suggested above or ask for advice from a senior person in HR, or at the school, club or workplace. A great new real-time resource is workbuddycheck.com.

At the end of this checkpoint you will see a few worksheets to dive into. The Pledge Worksheet—How are you going to show up for yourself and put your oxygen mask on first? The Traffic Light Worksheet that will help you assess where you sit in your life right now from super stressful to ok and manageable (i.e., green, amber and in the red zone).

Going through this worksheet and putting notes down takes the hectic overthinking energy away and gives you an anchor for conversations and shifting from chaos to calm. You'll also find a list of the signs of overwhelm to help you better understand where you sit right now.

- Check the lists of overwhelm signs and mark off ones that relate to you at this point.
- Be aware of triggers that make you feel nervous, anxious or afraid to be transparent—especially people, projects or even certain environments.
- Listen to the conversations you are having with yourself and take note of whether you are being judgemental, or shaming or blaming others.

- Take a deep breath and know this tiny shift in coordinates is the very first step towards putting you back in the driver's seat.

But before we get to the worksheets, let me introduce you to Jake Edwards and his journey from hero to having to reach out before it was too late.

A lot has changed in the area of mental health in recent years. As our awareness of this growing problem deepens, the stigma is slowly shifting and more and more business leaders, sports stars and other high achievers are opening up about their personal struggles and the heavy weight of expectations on their shoulders.

Jake's story is all about owning and taking responsibility for your mental health. It's about showing up for yourself and understanding that that is a sign of strength, not weakness.

PIT STOP WITH JAKE EDWARDS

'I grew up in a footy family, with the legacy of a long line of successful, professional players inspiring me to take to the field, so pursuing a career in football seemed like the obvious choice for me.

I had huge shoes to fill, and the stakes were enormous. I had spent so much time training and honing my football skills, but I was completely unprepared for how emotionally challenging it would be. I got to the point where I felt as though I was drowning under the weight of all these expectations, and anxiety, depression and addiction began to rule my life.

I did a great job of keeping up appearances. I pushed those negative feelings and self-talk to the back of my mind and put on a performance as the strong, capable guy. But that didn't fix what was going on inside my head. My thoughts grew darker and stronger, no matter how hard I tried to bury them.

It was all those unpleasant emotions that none of us like to confront: shame, guilt, and fear. These irrational feelings were never too far from the surface. The whole time, I avoided discussing my feelings with anyone. I hadn't told friends or family, so I was going through it all completely alone.

When you've been dealing with depression or extreme anxiety, it's not as simple as "bouncing back". It's not a visible scar or a broken arm; people can't see that you're hurt and need care and attention. You need to reach out and ask for help. It's hard but so important.

I also learned that you can't escape your truth, so the best solution is to embrace it. It's amazing how liberating that is.

Then, by sharing this with those around you, you're able to build a solid foundation and a game plan to get yourself back on the path to healing.

When you own your truth, no one can knock you over from that.

Looking after your own mental health is a real learning curve, because it's about more than simply attending counselling or taking medication.

Your mental state is often reflective of your physical state, so you need to be eating healthy food, exercising and creating a positive routine that leaves time for creative outlets and mindfulness. Take the time to plan your week and know your limits.

Figure out what you've got going on with work, your personal life and how you'll fit in that vital self-care.

Self-discipline is important, but so too is having quality coaches and a good support team around you who you really trust. You'll receive all kinds of advice, but try to listen to those who actually walk the walk. If someone around you is struggling with their mental health, it's okay to not know what to say. What matters is that you're there for them and you've got their back.'

CHECKPOINT 1 WORKSHEETS

THE PLEDGES

HOW WILL YOU
SHOW UP FOR
YOURSELF

TAKE THIS TIME NOW TO THINK ABOUT THE WAYS IN WHICH YOU ARE GOING TO TAKE CARE OF YOURSELF AND PUT YOUR OXYGEN MASK ON FIRST

I WILL PUT MY OXYGEN MASK ON FIRST AND COMMIT TO THE FOLLOWING:

THE TRAFFIC LIGHT WORKSHEET™

Drop the pin on what is in flow and where the biggest anxiety/stress and roadblocks sit. Be 100% honest.

GREEN (IN FLOW)	AMBER (ON THE EDGE)	RED (OVERDRIVE/OVERLOAD)

MENTAL

Where am I right now on this date - how am I feeling,

EMOTIONAL

Where am I right now on this date - how am I feeling,

PHYSICAL

Where am I right now on this date - how am I feeling,

"FEAR VERSUS CURIOSITY YOU CHOOSE"

-Nikki

2

CHECKPOINT
AWARENESS
TAKE YOUR
POWER BACK

awareness

/əˈwɛːnəs/

noun: awareness; plural noun: awarenesses

knowledge or perception of a situation or fact

synonyms: consciousness, recognition, realisation, cognisance,
perception, apprehension, understanding
grasp, appreciation, acknowledgement, knowledge
sensitivity to, sensibility to, insight into, familiarity with,
acquaintance with

opposite: ignorance

Welcome to Checkpoint 2: Awareness. This covers the ability to go within and be self-aware. It is learning that by hitting pause and switching on awareness, you can choose not to be trapped by the patterns and programming of the past. This checkpoint is about training you to feel the calm and quiet of inner knowing and then building on that experience.

It offers the opportunity to learn how to make decisions from trust, not terror.

Overwhelm, stress, anxiety, fear and panic all override our personal GPS and cause a sense of chaos, a feeling of being unanchored, and severely reduce our decision-making abilities. How you navigate this life and all of the conditions faced is your choice. It is how you utilise your mind, body, soul and connection that creates the results.

Here is a pivotal pit stop: how to truly shift from chaos to calm. In this checkpoint, we cover the following.

- **Programming:** Perception versus Reality. What if they were perceptions based on faulty programming and how to reset your inner GPS?
- **Patterns and Discernment:** How to discern the inner critic from the inner self. To pause the doubt and fear, instead regain a sense of self and get grounded at lightning speed.
- **Being on Purpose. Direction:** To understand the three vital and immediate steps you can do at any moment to bring yourself back into the present and apply the NOW, THEN and NEXT trilogy.
- **Being Present:** What we think about expands. Are you aware of your inner dialogue and what your body is trying to tell you?

You have a choice. Which voice do you follow: the inner critic or the intuition? Awareness of that inner critic (ego) versus our intuition (self) is that first step in the shift from chaos to calm.

If you don't create that choice to shift, you will stay stuck. Note that this does not require any action; it requires observation from a neutral position. I call it "OWLING".[11] It is observing one's thoughts, reactions, emotional and physical state. It is multidimensional, and it is the ability to connect with self, situation and senses at any given moment. It is an incredible skill we all need to master.

Life is purely about perspective. What is your reality?

I like to use the LION analogy—how two people can see a lion walking past them but have completely different reactions.

They might be frightened or curious, depending on their perception, exposure and inquisitiveness. One man sees a lion coming towards him and screams, runs and tries to hide. The other sits calmly, observing the majesty of nature, understanding this lion can outrun him, and remembers to stay calm and still in the face of adversity.

Same landscape, two different approaches.

Let's dive right in.

---

11 The Owling technique from QDM Coaching Program™ with Nikki.

"
IF YOU FIGHT FOR YOUR LIMITING BELIEFS, YOU WILL GET TO KEEP THEM

"

PROGRAMMING
(What is Your Perspective)

Are you hell-bent on not repeating the past? On trying to avoid conflict, and financial, personal, physical and emotional pain and loss? Moving from the work we did on vulnerability and recognising the signs of overwhelm (in Checkpoint 1: Survival mode), now we look deeper into the daily tools to step out of judgement and procrastination, or deflecting the blame.

A vital tool to enjoy this high-performing, ever-changing, digitally-transformed world we work and live in is true consciousness. It means shutting off the external influences for a moment and connecting to self. It is a sense of awareness.

- What if you could re-program and let go of outdated beliefs and operating systems and not lose yourself in the process?
- What if you could back yourself and start to rise above the self-doubt or guilt that is keeping you stuck in the past and the stories that block your future?
- What if you could truly pay attention to the now?

Fear of change is often the biggest handbrake for happiness. It is what holds us back from what great could really look like.

Overwhelm, overload, and the fear of being judged can create a debilitating inability to move forward, to acknowledge and honour what is really going on. It is being programmed from a young age to not disappoint, to always be enough and to do the right thing. That small mental limitation prevents many of us from harnessing the art of trying, crashing, refining and trying again.

Take a moment to stop and think about times when you may have been reprimanded for doing something by a parent, teacher, boss or friend and, therefore, been made to feel ashamed.

If you close your eyes for a moment, each of you reading this, no matter where you sit in life's journey, will be able to recognise the very earliest memory of being told one or more of the following:

'You should be ashamed of yourself.'

'Stop being so selfish.'

'Don't speak until you're spoken to.'

'Can't you just be like all of the others and/or just try to fit in?'

'You and your "imagination" again—I need you to concentrate.'

'Sorry, but no—what I say goes.'

'Don't think you'll ever be good enough to deserve that.'

'Money doesn't grow on trees.'

'Who's going to trust your crazy ideas?'

'Stop being so dramatic.'

and so on

It is crucial to truly understand the internal conversations, considerations and control mechanisms we have inherited through generations and our own youth to adulthood. These programs and patterns have shaped the decisions we have made up until now. You can't navigate the future until you clearly understand and make peace with the past.

Staying stuck in survival mode can have a lot to do with feeling like we have failed in some way or another. Blame, shame, fear and guilt. Failed who, I ask?

Much of this internal conflict is caused by past conditioning around shame (all factored with blame, guilt and fear).

shame

shame /ʃeɪm/

noun

painful feeling of humiliation or distress caused by the consciousness of wrong or foolish behaviour

synonyms: humiliation, mortification, chagrin, ignominy, loss of face, shamefacedness, embarrassment, indignity, abashment, discomfort, discomfiture, discomposure

make (someone) feel ashamed

synonyms: humiliate, mortify, make someone feel ashamed, chagrin, embarrass, abash, chasten, humble, put someone in their place, take down a peg or two, cut down to size, show up

Our first bust-up has a residual effect.

It is due to programming that we often have a deep and often misguided reaction to situations, people, places and circumstances that send us into a need to avoid pain. Is it possible that the fears holding you back are based on a misinterpretation of reality?

Our bodies harbour a chemical energy that is built up from the very first moment there was a 'bust-up'. This is usually where the EGO is formed, when you're told off for something—shamed, blamed, guilted, silenced, betrayed or berated. 'It's not good enough/you're not good enough.' Part of growing up. That tiny tiny moment has left a mark. It has created an internal hard-drive reflex to people, places or things that may disrupt the effort to maintain the status quo.

It creates a trauma bond.

Everybody has that first memory of being 'put in your place', whether right or wrong. There is an event that kicked it all off— when curiosity was replaced by fear. We can spend most of our lives unknowingly trying to stop this happening again. It is the subconscious mind 'protecting' us from another yuck feeling— usually shame, blame, guilt, fear or betrayal.

For many, it could also mean absolute terror.
Has it ever occurred to you that your view of yourself is just your perception of you formed by others' comments over time? What if I told you that you're judging yourself too harshly? What if you could stop a moment, turn on your awareness, and realise you don't have to try so hard?

When we free ourselves of shame and also stop inadvertently placing shame on others, we are able to operate at a whole other, higher and clearer level. But it isn't as easy as just flicking a switch. You need to be aware of it first and consciously choose to remove shame as an emotional anchor.

This is a good time to take a personal pit stop and do some writing with pen and paper about your personal journey so far. Consider past programming and patterns in limiting beliefs and the little voice that holds you back without you even realising it. I ask all my clients to write a full letter to their younger self with as much detail as they can remember (bullet points or prose, it doesn't matter).

Where can you remember feeling shame yourself, judged or blamed? And then, also, where do you remember you may have judged, shamed and blamed others? This was perhaps not done maliciously, but even so, it is important to recognise both when you do this inventory around vulnerability, fear, blame, shame and guilt.

Feeling ashamed of yourself (judging self):

This can be deeply set from your childhood, when you were told off for the first time or made to feel embarrassed about an innocent action. This can hardwire a set of beliefs that you are not good enough or that what you do is never going to be good enough, regardless of what you are doing or striving for.

Putting a feeling of shame onto others (judging others):

You may not even realise you are doing this, but by not accepting people as they are, by using certain language, by looking down on others and by voicing your opinion as if it's the only way to see the world, you can cause an extraordinary amount of shame in others.

Whatever we judge in others is a direct reflection of the work we must do for ourselves. So, observe the above two filters. Write out the moments and the memories, the names or the instances and realise that you can release these past experiences—with forgiveness and understanding.

If you think about some of the judgements you may have heard as a child or criticism that may have been harmless at the time (as per our little notes and review in Checkpoint 1 on limiting beliefs), then it is quite possible the GPS you have been using to make your decisions and navigate through this crazy fast-paced world does not represent the best coordinates.

- Are you leaning on a false sense of security? Are you proudly pushing through, putting up with and surviving against all odds?
- Each day, each week, each month are you sacrificing your truth and happiness to keep up appearances and avoid conflict? Is the thought of change so frightening that it's better to stay stuck in what you know, even if it is causing you great discomfort?

Whoever said that brute force, pushing through challenges and anxiety-led decisions was the way we determine our roadmap for success?

- Where was it written that 'hard work' meant the trip to the top would probably cause horrendous collateral damage— divorce, depression, disillusionment and distrust?
- Where can you see the patterns of comparison, the judgement that whatever you're doing is not enough or perhaps that you're not enough?

PATTERNS

Whatever your upbringing, whether you had everything or you had nothing, those are the two defining, polarising characteristics. The important element is you understand the patterns at play in your day.

Regardless of the circumstances, there will be patterns at play as a result of programming, and these patterns are the key to unlock your true potential and find your glide in life. You just have to be willing to lean in a little and really be willing to choose curiosity over fear.

Often the biggest roadblock in our life is actually our own mindset. You know that you're a capable, intelligent, driven, fantastic human. So, where does the doubt come in? When is the last time you fully trusted yourself on a deep, gut level—no questions, just pure belief in an idea, a decision and a moment?

Understanding where you have been making your decisions in life is important. By avoiding change and growth for fear of where it may take us (a.k.a. the unknown), we stay in a mental prison and put up barriers to true happiness. We have patterns to 'prevent us from pain'. This, in turn, shows itself via these behaviours:
- being emotionally unavailable,
- being too busy to work on self,
- avoiding love (of people, places and things),
- experiencing purpose-work procrastination (doing everything BUT what you would love to do),
- hoping someone else will make a decision so you don't have to,
- rejecting joy in case it doesn't last (if I don't have it, I can't lose it),
- engaging in passive or aggressive conversation styles,
- permitting codependency, and
- pushing for martyrdom.

"YOUR EGO IS NOT YOUR AMIGO

-Nikki

"

 RADICAL SELF BELIEF

BEING ON PURPOSE: DISCERNMENT

Being authentic with yourself first is often the hardest part, but it is the most rewarding. The first step to this is having the awareness to discern between the inner critic and your true inner self. You can then choose who to listen to. This is a minute-by-minute practice—there is no magic switch. You must be impeccable with the self-discipline around your thoughts, as they determine your actions and the outcomes around you.

Rather than making decisions from the busy mind, which generates anxiety, doubt and confusion, slowly build the ability to listen to your true guide instead of your patterned, programmed conversation. It takes much more energy to live in fear, doubt and over rationalisation than it does to live from conviction and calm. Mastering self is part of navigating our high-performance world.

Which voice are you listening to: fear or curiosity?

Our ego puts up barriers for change, as it thinks it is protecting us from hurt, loss, failure, pain, grief, shame, blame and guilt. But you have to know the difference. You need discernment.

Are you aware of the stories you tell yourself?
- Who do you listen to the most in your decision-making: your head or your heart?
- Can you discern the difference between ego and self?

We are trained to 'not get too excited' about a positive thing, to 'soldier on and not give up', that 'everything worth having is only possible through hard work'. We are taught to wear suffering, working long hours, being 'busy' and feeling exhausted like a badge of honour.

- Always give 100%
- NEVER give up
- Being rich is ostentatious
- Not pretty enough, smart enough, good enough
- If you don't sweat and work for everything, you are nothing
- Emotions are weakness
- You are defined by your work
- No pain, no gain
- Don't talk about work at home

This is the guilt and over-giving, never-enough trap. Selfishness, sacrifice and martyrdom. Fear, anger, grief and disappointment like to hang out with each other in a glorious pity party, locking the door to any joy, harmony or success. These emotions hold you ransom to the past, perpetuate your fear of failure and rejection and encourage you to repeat past mistakes.

Does your mind keep you busy with all sorts of overthinking? Is that little voice trying to convince you that the brief moments of shining/happiness/success are 'a fluke, it won't last'?

Our clever subconscious mind works insidiously in the background. It fools us into believing we are doing well, then sabotages any true sustainable success by throwing in doubt, fear and guilt, or convincing us that great things and moments won't last.

We have to continually recognise the limiting beliefs that sit there quietly in the background, waiting for their chance to override faith. Having access to your true conscious self and getting off autopilot is imperative.

This is by choice, not chance. When we weave through this stage, this foundation work sets up the strength to underpin your mental and physical wellbeing. It provides an extremely valuable set of tools that helps you to stop BEFORE there is too much dust on the windscreen.

Without clear vision, we quickly go down bumpy roads. The irony is that the choices you have been making may have been fuelled by your subconscious (ego) instead of self (true intuition).

What's your mental diet? How you talk to yourself really matters. Is that incredible amount of non-stop internal chatter in your head driving you crazy?

- Does it keep trying to convince you to be less bold and courageous, and more worried about what others may think?
- Does it tell you to hold back on sharing thoughts, goals, ideas and feelings in case they're judged or rejected?
- Does it have you questioning your experience, your great work ethic, or your ability to have, do and be ANYTHING you put your mind to?

We are so hard on ourselves, let alone the expectations we may (unjustly) place on others—the real struggle is the one within. 'I'm not good enough, it's not good enough, it's never enough.'

Ego versus Self

Everyone has an ego. Mine happens to be called 'Bob' (it always helps to name your ego/subconscious voice). That's the name I gave my inner chatter, so I know when he's around and can tell him quite firmly to be quiet.

It's vital in life to distinguish between your EGO and your INTUITION. Self is extremely powerful and the ego is a saboteur. Self connects you to your best path, while the ego tries to get you to take the long way around and avoid risks.

Ego is governed by fear and failure and Self is driven by conviction and connection.

Can you hear yourself and the negative self-talk that goes on?

They are two completely separate entities but also part of who we are. Embrace that knowledge. You can't remove fears and doubts completely, but you can be aware of their origin and consciously choose the thoughts you use as anchors in your day.

You may need to silence that little voice in your head and try following your heart this week, in leadership and in life.

The first thought is habit, the second one is your choice. Stop and recognise that you're heating up before it gets out of control—hear yourself before you react, speak and respond to a situation. Then pause to reflect. Is this a major issue? Am I just a little over-tired and not present?

First of all, here's how to discern the difference. Choose your thoughts as they determine your reality.

EGO (SELF-TALK) Noisy and distracting	Insert a positive comment here	SELF-(CENTRED) Peaceful and calm
The Ego usually poses a bunch of questions as answers, creating a feeling of confusion and doubt.	One that shows up for you, believes in you, says 'I can', 'it is', 'I will'. Locked and loaded in clarity and calm.	The Self focuses on simple 'yes', 'no', 'this feels right', 'this is right', 'this is not feeling right'. Less confusion and a quiet clarity.
REPLACE THIS	**WITH THIS**	**TO ACHIEVE THIS**
Discontented/ restless/anxious/ worried		Clarity
Disconnected from what you feel, say, do		At peace with yourself and trusting decisions
Good doesn't last, positive is temporary		Acknowledges feelings and can identify why
Pain is normal		Confidently value yourself and others
You have to be prepared to lose something to get something		Effortless and easy is the norm
Hard work pays off, so suck it up and push through		Self-care is a priority so that you can be there for others
It's normal to sacrifice		Confident in the value you offer others
I have to please everyone		In your truth— centred and calm

Confusion, lacking direction/indecisive		• It gives you a direction, a purpose and a sense of true north.
• Ha ha, you really think you can do that?		• It's a feeling first. Not a bunch of chatter. It's the calm and rational voice.
• Don't bother applying for that.		• It's the KNOWING.
• Do you think they're even going to notice you?		• It's feeling connected.
• Who's going to read that?		• Grounded.
• Wearing a suit doesn't make you deserve a seat at this table.		• Stable.
• You can work out later—you're having way too much fun, come on and live a little.		It's the VERY FIRST thought that comes into your head when you take time out to pause quietly and ask an important question.
• So, you think you can start your own business? Good luck, buddy.		It's your inner compass

- What are the family going to think?

It's the self-belief, determination and grit that makes you who you are.

- Who's really your friend anyway?

It's often the quietest voice in your head, but the strongest feeling in your gut and in your heart.

BASE EMOTIONS		
I WANT TO PREVENT (SUBCONSCIOUS DECISION-MAKING FROM FEAR)	INSTEAD I WANT TO FEEL (REPLACE FEAR WITH CONSCIOUS, CURIOSITY-BASED INTENT)	AS A RESULT, I HAVE (CONSCIOUS OUTCOME)
Shame, judgement		Courage
Blame		Pride
Guilt		Purpose
Fear		Passion
Loss, rejection, abandonment		Love
		Understanding
		Compassion

BEING PRESENT—MASTERING TRIGGERS, MIRRORING AND DEFLECTION

When you start to feel overwhelm kick in or anxiety, fear, panic and the busy subconscious mind, remember to take these three immediate steps towards awareness:

- **Breathe:** The fastest way to get connected to self and stop a panic attack is to concentrate on your breathing. Slowly and surely.
- **Focus:** Shift your perception—fear to curiosity.
- **Direct:** Define what the one NEXT best thing to do is, without creating ten further actions that prevent you from doing just one action.

Think of this as a toolkit to immediately regain a sense of sovereign control, no matter what is going on around you. It is like a pit stop for your mind.

We only get triggered by what we are lacking in ourselves. So, as you go about your day, be aware of your triggers:

- **your internal ego**—the busy conversation and perceived roadblocks (fears, doubts, shame, blame, questioning); and
- **the external triggers**—the people, places and things that show you what you need to look at and let go of.

On this note, I want to highlight the importance of understanding how we can get triggered by others. It takes skill and awareness to be truly accountable; to not react to others behaviours, but instead see any trigger as a gift for growth in ourselves. We are a projection of our inner thoughts and fears, so that is why mirroring is so insightful.

Recognise that being triggered by others is an opportunity for your own personal growth. A judgement or criticism of others is usually reflecting a deficit in our own values, self-worth or behaviour. As the saying goes, 'one finger pointing out, three fingers pointing back at you'. And it's so, so true.

This analogy is really important to understand. It means that every time we point the finger and blame someone else, or judge another, there are actually three fingers pointing back at us. Other people's behaviours that annoy you are usually triggers for you to look at what you can do for yourself.

It could be around their spending, their courage to present themselves in a meeting, ask for a promotion, drive a fancy car, be outspoken, wear something different or one of myriad things!

So, what can you do? Instead of reacting, recognise that feeling of judgement or frustration, then pause and ask yourself: 'What actions am I not following through or how am I not in alignment? What does this mean for me?'

Are you getting super annoyed at people around you not making decisions, staying stuck, talking about the same issues over and over again, not taking opportunities, or choosing to stay in unhealthy but familiar patterns rather than taking steps to move away from them?

If you are, this is probably a direct reflection of what action you are not taking in your own life. Stop looking out for validation and get the conversation with yourself right first.

Often, we subconsciously sabotage our growth and success by helping out with other people, projects, places and things instead of focusing on our true north.

AWARENESS IS A DAILY PRACTICE

Notice if you are projecting—that is, blaming—others' reactions for your self-doubt or wobbly moments when you are pursuing something you are passionate about. If external energies affect you that much, it means you are not centred enough in your own self and idea to back it.

Peacefulness comes from knowing that you don't need to be all things for all people. You need to do the work yourself.

If you don't use these tools of self-awareness to get out of self-doubt, feeling inadequate, imposter syndrome and being 'the black sheep', then you'll stay locked in that mindset of lack/fear and judgement. The trick is to pause and catch that first blurt.

Create a speech bubble in your head, recognise that is your ego talking, and push it aside like the NEO in the movie The Matrix. Then choose your next thought carefully and with intent. Be present and on purpose.

So, as you wander around your days, notice if you are doing distraction tactics—that is, pouring yourself into someone's problems but ignoring your own. What are you really avoiding thinking about? This is your life—now. This is your work day to organise, your company to run and your relationship to show up in. Stop blaming others for what's not working out and start asking yourself, 'What can I do better, clearer, smarter and be more open about?'

The next time someone does something to upset you or let you down, ask yourself what you really needed in the first place and if you are prepared to be clear, have conviction and communicate that need in a way that others can understand.

What story are you hanging on to that no longer serves you?
- Whose voice(s) are you listening to that really have no idea how to even begin to achieve what you have in mind—even if it's as simple as redefining your work-life blend?
- What past experiences are anchoring you and holding you back from trusting? You're not the same person you were five years, months or even weeks ago. If you're 'woke' as they say, then you're constantly evolving.

Unveil these roadblocks/insights and triggers by writing them down (you will notice the EGO BLURTS worksheet at the end of this checkpoint to train you to do just that).

We all do it. Are you unknowingly repeating programming with your family, staff, and so on by using patterns based on people-pleasing and not standing in clear communication? Are you expecting validation for doing the right thing but never feeling fulfilled, then wondering why that cycle perpetuates?

I know that it can be so easy to throw a pity party when things don't feel like they are going your way: 'not again, I can't take another blow, nothing works out, this is doomed, I am doomed.' But it's time to stop that cycle. It is destructive, exhausting and counterproductive. Allowing fear to dominate will keep you exactly where you are right now. It will keep you stuck.

Avoiding pain by staying stuck keeps us in unhealthy relationships at work and at home, and ultimately in an unhealthy relationship with yourself.

Lack of action is itself an action. If you keep making the same mistakes, chances are you're not learning from them and trying something different. If you don't want to repeat patterns and perceived 'failures', then it's time to step up and out of the old story and start writing the new one.

> *Freedom for every man and every woman lies in the mind's ability to alter old habits.*
>
> -DON MIGUEL RUIZ

It is empowering to identify that your past/subconscious programming is holding you back, that you may be leaning away from your greatest abundance because you are frightened of change.

Observe what your thoughts are focusing on, what/who frustrates you, where you need to hear 'how' you may be thinking, and make a conscious choice to change that internal pattern.

Awareness is a gift we can call upon naturally. However, this awareness, or mindfulness, is not just something you do when you meditate. In fact, it is the crucial co-factor in all areas of our life for ultimate success. It is the very art of being present, of being able to observe before reacting or responding. It is the moment we get to choose—consciously.

Always stop and write things down. Winners do not wing it. Do so on a minute-by-minute basis when you're having days where you are triggered, challenged and feeling out of alignment.

Have a go at what I call 'owling' this week: Instead of reacting, or responding, just observe. Is it really as bad as you think?

Make notes. Don't just reflect mentally, but take the time to write this down on your phone or notebook. I usually recommend pen and paper, as it has a direct cognitive decluttering effect in our brain. But anything will work, as long as you can actually note these elements and self-reflections. It's super important not to let that energy float around in the much-needed mental hard-drive space.

Identifying roadblocks, triggers and blurts on paper diffuses the negative energy of thoughts in our head.

"DON'T JUST THINK IT, INK IT"

-Nikki

SET YOUR INTENT

I always say to my clients, 'Your deep self knows where it is going—I'm just the navigator lighting one row on the runway at a time'.

Once you begin to master discernment between subconscious, limiting beliefs and your quieter, centred, real truth, you can start to put direction into play.

It is important to understand that self-belief is not created in a single moment. You can't just say it once and become magically transformed into a lighter, higher being. Self-doubt is like a fire—it needs oxygen to expand and grow. Don't feed it.

We may read 'believe in yourself', 'you are your greatest asset' and other, similar inspiring quotes as they pop up on news feeds, in conferences and leadership mindfulness training. The challenge is how to actually do that consistently.

> *Progress. Not perfection.*

Keep reminding yourself that life is about progress, not perfection. Nothing is perfect—life is organic. Trying to control everything and everyone around you will send you into a tailspin. Recognise that you may feel at times powerless over the limiting beliefs, destructive ego and busy mind when it keeps you up at night, churning around and making you feel off-centre, unsure and disconnected from your truth and clarity.

We can't remove our ego or those outdated programs that formed much of our internal dialogue as we were growing up or building our life—they will always sit there like old folders in a cloud-storage system. But we can stop for a moment in awareness, question whether they are real or just an outmoded perception, use our discernment to answer that question, and then set a new direction.

The truth is, you absolutely have the ability to redirect your thoughts and take a shift—just five degrees left or right.

WHAT NOW?

What is the next best step to take? Do the work around awareness. Once you understand there is an inner critic versus inner self, the next step is to apply this understanding and work on being fully aware.

As we move from awareness mode into stepping up and defining your truth, take a moment to cement these observations. Remember to apply the work here, minute by minute and day by day:

- recognise the programming,
- be on purpose with the thoughts you choose, and
- be present to observe before you react to life.

Don't give self-doubt and negative self-talk any energy. The way to do that is to acknowledge that thought, then let it go and choose your own true inner wish, need or want. The truth. Have a bit of a laugh at yourself. 'There's that negative old pattern again—ha ha—well, I choose not to give it any weight or meaning.'

Trust yourself and your intuition. This is a new feeling for many. When you're in the flow, there's no other way to go. It feels right. It makes you energised. You're heading in the right direction.

It can make you feel isolated at first, as you may grow past those you know. That's okay. For top leadership in life, vision is crucial for growth. Staying stuck in the past can prevent your incredible future if you're not willing to give up your fear and trust your insight.

Positive mental attitude takes training. If you reflect, you have probably spent most of your life flexing your deep subconscious muscles by living according to external rules and not really being in tune with your inner needs, wants and wishes.

The quick chemistry check:
1. accept there's an issue or misalignment;
2. acknowledge where that is coming from;
3. adapt your thinking to be centred in self, not self-talk; and
4. identify and write down triggers and blurts that will diffuse their perceived power.

Moving from ego to conscious decision-making will take practice and a new sense of direction. The world's best athletes invest in mental training as well as physical—so why don't we?

Sure, many of us are not brought up to be daredevils, rally drivers or champion tennis players, but what I would like to remind you about any athlete is that they are dedicated to all aspects. They don't wing it.

They do the work, they prepare, they lean into the corners and they are acutely aware of their breath, their focus and the next right thing to do. Then, they just go for it. They don't let fear hold them back as they use the tools to get centred and cut out all of the white noise, the old programming. They stop, breathe, focus and take the next step.

Recognise when you're out of flow and how to realign with the right path when it feels like you might 'lose it all' in the process. What if this idea of yours could work out? What if you could re-shape elements of your life and business based on 'downloads' of what may be truly special and exciting to you?

Once you realise that purging the old makes room for new elements that are important for intellectual and emotional growth—better insights, feelings and positive beliefs—you'll wish you'd discovered this earlier.

I challenge you today to stop overthinking and going around and around in circles. Instead, gather the simple, straightforward facts, then take a moment to pause. Block out the white noise: the 'shoulds', 'coulds', 'should haves', 'this didn't work before', 'that didn't happen for me', and so on.

Do the worksheets, use the frameworks on the back of a napkin or a scrap piece of paper when you start to understand how valuable these pit stops are.

At the end of this chapter you will find a couple of worksheets. The first EGO/BLURTS has two columns representing the 'wants and why nots'. The A column is 'needs and desires' and the B column is 'blurts and blocks', which pop up as you dare to define what happiness looks like for you.

The other worksheet is the ANCHORING WORKSHEET, The 4 Checkpoints—the NOW, THEN, NEXT & IF. This is a great technique to anchor immediate steps and actions, without letting the fear of not having it all figured out stop you from making just one step in the right direction.

Change the lens.

You are in the driver's seat. You can't control your first thought, as it can come from deep programming, but you do have a choice with what you instil in yourself and your mindset with your second. What thoughts will you anchor to?

> "
> *No entrepreneurial life or any kind of life should be filled with anxiety, overwhelm and depression. You do not need to accept that as the flip side of success.*[12]
> "

---

12 Brad Feld, Inc. Magazine.

Please stop judging yourself and others and have an open mind. When you see other people's lives only through this veil of perfection, it can leave you feeling manifestly inadequate. But this vulnerability is not a weakness. It's a powerful part of our journey and it makes us who we are.

Importantly, know when it's time to pull up the handbrake. It might be as little as five minutes to recalibrate, but give yourself permission to take that time. Take time to do the mental pit stop. As world-renowned yogi Andrea Marcum explains, you don't need all the equipment, the supplements, the courses, the books. All you need is the positive intention to take a step up, find your true self and discover what makes your heart sing.

" EVOLUTION, NOT RESOLUTION "

-Nikki

PIT STOP WITH ANDREA MARCUM

'In yoga, there's a concept known as perusha. It's all about finding your true self. Not the front you put up or the blemish-free aspects of your life you post on social media, but your true self.

Real life shares a lot of parallels with yoga. When you fall out of a pose, you learn more than when you float effortlessly into it, and the same applies to your personal and professional life. Our flaws and mistakes make us equal parts vulnerable and fascinating, and all of this is built on the connections we make.

When you truly connect with yourself, your environment and the people around you, you're more effective and progressive. After all, there's nothing brave or courageous about leaving a comment online with nothing at stake. Opening up to real-world connections brings accountability for how we show up for ourselves, our work, our friends and families, and the planet. That's so powerful.

A lot of people are under the misguided belief that mindfulness and meditation are about tuning out, but they couldn't be more wrong.

It's about tuning in, pausing to take a breath and being comfortable with being still in the moment.

For example, I'm sure you've been in a meeting or conversation when there has been a pause and everyone scrambles over themselves to fill it up with noise. Instead of reacting and defaulting to that knee-jerk reaction, why not give ourselves the

time and space to really respond, to digest what is going on, consider it carefully and feed this into our intent going forward. When we're always going, going, going, we're constantly running on cortisol, like hamsters in a wheel. It's what we've been taught, it's all we know—but it's not the only way.

Take a conscious breath within the space available to you, and let it energise you so you can lengthen and expand, then contract and find your roots again—that's how we nurture sustainable, effective growth.

It can be as simple as just moving and getting started. It doesn't have to be big or exotic, just open your eyes to what is around you and be willing to receive it. Take manageable steps, modify and implement changes as you go, and give yourself the space to feel those little wins. When you feel the rewards, you'll want to keep trying, instead of forcing yourself to carry on. You won't want to self-sabotage, because you're so connected to yourself and your purpose.

These days, we're surrounded by disconnection and false connections, and while technology certainly has a place in our life, it's a lot like fire.

Sure, it can help you cook, warm your home, illuminate the night, but it can also burn and destroy. We need to find that balance.

Instead of Facetime, spend real time.

Don't be so busy posting photos of your food that you forget to savour the tastes and textures that are in front of you.

Stop focusing on sharing and liking everything, and love and live instead.

Come face to face with yourself, and confront your personal challenges and difficulties.

Every challenge is an opportunity to learn, grow and be humbled.

Sometimes we step into the ocean and it's deeper than we anticipated. It's then that we have two choices: we can either give up and never go back, or keep going and discover that side of ourselves that we've been searching for.'

CHECKPOINT 2 WORKSHEETS

THE BLURTS (EGO)

WORKSHEET

Understanding the difference between your core wants and the blurts come up as you start to get centred in self

THE A COLUMN - WHAT I REALLY WANT

Write the now and next, the ideas, the outcomes, the results what ever it is you want to have, feel and think is crucial for you without any filter. What is for your highest good?

_____
_____
_____
_____
_____

THE B COLUMN - BLURTS (WHY NOT)

Write the blurts, counter thoughts, limiting beliefs, fears of what could happen or who would respond negatively. All the things that come up when you write out what you really want - what's stopping you?

_____
_____
_____
_____
_____

THE 4 CHECKPOINTS™

– identify where you are now, what needs to happen and the next steps after that. Place the 'if' scenarios in their own section so all actions and ideas have a relevant time and place to be focused upon

THE NOW

What are the immediate actions, questions, desired outcomes - the must do, have, say, action

ANSWER

THE WHAT IF?

Write the blurts, the concerns, the unknown factors and the questions you can't answer or bigger variables here.

ANSWER

THE THEN

Identify the actions, questions, desired outcomes that would follow or can be done once step NOW is complete

WHAT IS THE NEXT

Write the question you want to ask your students and allot space for the answers.

" COURAGE, DARE TO DEFINE "

-Nikki

3

CHECKPOINT
ACCOUNTABILITY

HOW TO OWN
YOUR SIDE OF
THE STREET

 RADICAL SELF BELIEF

accountability

/əˌkaʊntəˈbɪlɪti/

noun

the fact or condition of being accountable; responsibility

synonyms: responsibility, liability, answerability,
responsibility, reporting, obedience

This is the checkpoint that really creates the dynamic shift for people.

Accountability separates the wish list from the winning list. Many people spend years and years trying to discover the mental handbrakes, the core wounding and elements that create self sabotage, or the hidden subconscious mind that makes decisions from fear, shame, blame and guilt.

This is the true test of your willingness to move from staying stuck in pain and disillusionment to taking charge of your now and the future. We take a pit stop and dare to define our truth.

This will assist you in creating a conscious platform, a solid foundation from which you can set clear intent and be connected to your goals going forward.

Empowering you with this confidence will engage you mentally and emotionally to take action in your own life. It is very powerful and also very personal.

If you have done the work in Checkpoint 2, you will have created a benchmark of awareness that uncovers what programming may have been holding you back in your own journey. Perhaps these are outdated thought processes and belief systems you were not even aware of.

Let's reflect on what we have just worked through:

a. In survival mode, we must put our oxygen mask on first so that we are fully capable of undertaking the responsibilities and providing support to other people if we need to.

b. In awareness mode, we need to recognise our triggers and the times when we are deflecting. We do this by owning our own thoughts and actions, by not deflecting or being the problem solver for everyone else.

These two fundamental pit stops can be deployed through all the stages—at any given moment.

They provide you with the opportunity to be accountable for your words, actions and thoughts. Practise the ability to discern and stay grounded. Change is constant. How you show up in your life is what determines your results.

Checkpoint 3 is your chance to really suit up and show up for yourself. Remember the fundamentals. You can't skip steps— there is no bypass on this roadmap.

Instead, there is a proven framework that you must navigate one checkpoint at a time to create a genuine and solid foundation. Cement new habits, be present in any given moment—sharpen that essential peripheral vision.

As you navigate through Checkpoint 3, take your learnings from checkpoints 1 and 2. Keep your notes next to you as you remind yourself of the constant need to discern which voice you are listening to and whether there are signs that you are creeping back into overwhelm.

I'm going to keep this checkpoint pretty simple, as the proof will be in the work you do at the end to get prepared and grounded. It is our viewpoint and reaction to situations that determine how we travel this path.

We all know there are elements that we cannot change. We also are very aware that the true fundamental of accountability and adulting the rally of life is taking care of our side of the street before we worry about others.

In this checkpoint we will cover the following:

1. How to define your vital ingredients—what you really need to function at your personal best.
2. Honouring your truth—how to show up for yourself and communicate without conflict as you navigate the ever-changing landscape of our complex world and the challenges that come with that.

HOW TO DEFINE YOUR VITAL INGREDIENTS

As human beings, we all have different things that light us up and make us tick. Knowing the core ones and being able to identify them gives you a much higher chance of sustainable success. If you do not define what you want and need, then you will absolutely get what you are given.

What is your personal prescription for happiness, health and prosperity? What environments and ecosystems best suit you? Are you a morning person or an evening person? Mountains or ocean? Coffee or tea?

How can you integrate more of these elements into your days and weeks to create sustainable energy, harmony and success?

You don't put unleaded fuel in a diesel engine, so how are you fuelling your mind, body and soul each day?

I remember being told when I got my first car to never let the gas get down to empty and always make sure the oil levels were healthy. The first part of this checkpoint is to ensure you are correctly fuelled—mentally, physically and emotionally—for the rugged road ahead.

This requires you to clearly identify your vital ingredients.

"WINNERS DO NOT WING IT"

—Nikki

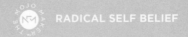

Knowing what is vital to you means owning your side of the street.

When you choose to be accountable to yourself, you start to put a positive course correction into play for your mental and physical wellbeing. That in turn will have a positive ripple effect in your core circle, finances and productivity.

What is the recipe for your sustainable success? It is one that allows you to be consistent—not experiencing extreme highs and lows, but truly knowing how to recharge and reconnect, and what is crucial for you to be clear-headed every day.

For many of you, this is the first time in a long time, if at all, that you will be taking time to really think about this and make your list without fear of judgement or being called selfish.

The issue is that many of us are conditioned to negotiate for our needs and wants from a very young age.

'If you eat all your vegetables, you can have an ice cream.'

'If I do this, can I stay up later?'

'What if I finish this part of the assignment and get the rest in by Monday, and I promise I will have it in before...'

It is essential that you take time to define your vital ingredients.

Plus, it is not only essential for your relationship with yourself, it's also a crucial element of any relationship with a partner/family or colleague. It is a co-requisite for being in the driver's seat.

For example, for me, I know that to deliver my very best work, support my incredible clients, feel happy, nurtured, energised and well, I need certain elements. The following are my vital ingredients:

- the ocean/water/nature/fresh air;
- seizing the day—I'm a morning person;
- a framework for values and vision alignment with my clients;
- fresh, healthy food;
- my Labrador, Roxy;
- an open-plan home that is bright and airy;
- time to myself to write, work on my projects, play guitar, skateboard, surf, swim, play whatever I feel like;
- driving a great car or just being around engines and boats—something I really love;
- laughter;
- working with intelligent and value-led people;
- going off-grid and having adventures;
- coffee;
- good quality, honest friendships;
- speaking to my parents whenever I can; and
- French champagne (just giving you all the details here).

Daring to define your vital ingredients is the very first step. Make choices about where you spend your time.

Don't avoid good things or good people because you're afraid they won't last.

Your vibe attracts your tribe; make a conscious effort to be aware of who you want to be surrounded by and why. Define what a great day looks like, then refine that definition so that key people in your life also understand the outline. We empower others to support our goals when we back them wholeheartedly.

HONOURING YOUR TRUTH

It is imperative that we follow through with our truth in all areas of our lives. But to do that you need to disassociate from the idea that doing so will mean conflict, because that makes you shut the idea down before you even bring it up. So, trust in this process and follow through for yourself.

At the end of this checkpoint there will be a worksheet for you to fill in so that you can do a pit stop and consider what your vital ingredients are. This is so that—like any good workshop for high-performance cars—we don't leave any part of the engine to chance.

Blurt Alert: If you can hear the blurts come up before you even start this exercise, then write them down! Do not ignore those triggers and signals that show you roadblocks to your true happiness. Bring them right up to the surface. Awareness 101 means no skipping the foundations.

Once we see the truth, we have the freedom to make a choice.

Hmmm, the million-dollar question: 'What do I want and need?' How do I really feel and what do I honestly think? No filters, just pure truth.

Can you answer that? Can you unearth the fear that is holding back so many people from stepping out of chaos and into a sense of self?

SHARING YOUR TRUTH

Old wounds or programs can create the fear of even thinking about voicing what you want. Part of this checkpoint—accountability—is communicating without conflict and teaching you the four key steps to honour your truth.

This is speaking up and putting yourself first in a healthy, assertive way. Creating change and taking a leap of faith to set your life on a better foundation does not need to be associated with conflict.

What if the people who were dear to you and important in your life were able to listen without prejudice? (I can hear you scoff as you read this, saying 'as if'). But bear with me for a second and just imagine that you can create a space where assertive, clear communication is the best option.

I think this is by far the hardest step for most stoic leaders I work with, as they usually take the path of least resistance just to avoid conflict. Over the years, they have often pushed down their wants and needs so they can be there for others or just to avoid arguments and discord.

What can go wrong with sharing what you want and need?

Before you defend the actions or position of the other person or parties involved, let's flip it around and pose this question: What if you could come into this next phase with curiosity rather than fear?

Somewhere, somehow, we have been conditioned to think that being centred in self is to be selfish and self-centred—and that speaking up is something to be admonished. With no limit in terms of race, age or gender, it seems to be inherent to many upbringings.

If you think back to your earliest memories, I am sure you can remember the first time you were scolded for being selfish, or told to wait and to 'put up with what you had', or admonished in some other way according to the belief system that was handed down to you at the time.

The whole point of this book is that now is the time to go from chaos to calm—and you're in charge of that shift. You must have the courage to define what it is that makes you happy and gather around you the tools and people that best align with who you are and what your values are.

There is no avoiding your core, grounded needs and wants any more. There is no hiding behind excuses or fearing the reactions of others. I am asking you here to suit up, buckle up, and go bush-crashing with a Polaris RZR[13]—not roam around a well-manicured golf course in a buggy.

What if you feel there is no way you can share this?

---

13   All-terrain vehicle.

Then you really need to go back over checkpoints 1 and 2. Put your oxygen mask on first. Be aware of what could be holding you back or pushing your basic happiness to the back of the line. Decide then that you are going to lead in your life.

1. If you are truly going to get out of the passenger's seat, reduce overwhelm and feel the freedom to express yourself and unlock your potential, then it is important you take the time to acknowledge these elements for you first.

2. Anyone who truly loves and supports you, someone who is an authentic mentor or a great manager, will absolutely want you to be your best self. I can only remind couples and leaders that interdependence is where amplification happens. You will have a happier, longer-lasting and more enriching relationship, whether it is work or at home, when you empower the other person to be their personal best and you can do the same.

DON'T DEVIATE FROM HONESTY WITH SELF AND OTHERS

I know this is a huge challenge. That is why we are doing the deeper work upfront. We should not build towers on quicksand. Being in the driver's seat will require you to have the awareness that people-pleasing, external validation and co-dependent cycles will come to an end naturally when you start to build a new, healthy framework for decision-making.

Think of your truth as building a really solid chassis on a vehicle that needs to go through all terrain and all conditions.

Your wellbeing and happiness are no one else's responsibility. They are your own. If you're stuck, take a moment to press pause and do the traffic-light check-in.

Check martyrdom levels if you were previously drawn to stories of suffering and keen to help others before you were grounded, and then make sure you are aware of the triggers for that.

Press pause for a second to answer some questions:
- Do you think it is healthy to be in a work or personal relationship that makes you feel that you have to push your needs and wants down and out of sight? Y/N
- Does identifying your vital ingredients—what you need to absolutely rock your world and bring your best—and voicing that list, empower you? Y/N
- Are you afraid to define this list because you want to avoid conflict, because it could cause a reaction that is so unstable that you would rather not mention it at all? Y/N
- Stop and consider—that environment, that feeling of being stuck in fear of the perceived reaction—would you want that for your best friend, or your son or daughter? Y/N

Of course not. So, it is time to be accountable to yourself. This is achieved by standing in your truth—no one can take that away from you. To have to negotiate and 'sell' an idea or need is extremely disempowering. We do not own, nor should we stake a claim to control, another person's road to happiness. And vice versa.

Do not let the perceived negative reaction of someone or something get in the way of the true possibility of a happy outcome.

Consider the vital-ingredients list and then use the four quadrants of conscious communication to create a simple framework. This will give you a clear and calm viewpoint to get your thoughts, needs, feelings and wants out on paper. It will give you a tool-kit for discussion with key stakeholders in your life.

I recommend testing out your truth matrix by running through your answers with a trusted source, colleague or friend. It's empowering and inspiring to others when you lead by example like that.

Before you think about your destination, the groundwork needs to be down on what really matters to you in the first place. Decision-making frameworks that will guide you under pressure need to be built.

To be in your sovereign self and in the driver's seat, you must have the courage to put these points—your vital ingredients, needs, wants and core considerations—to the people you love.

Trevor Hendy is a former champion Ironman turned motivational speaker. You don't succeed in elite sport without being accountable to yourself. So, let's hear a little bit about how he achieves that mindset.

PIT STOP WITH TREVOR HENDY

'When we talk about accountability, we're talking about embracing the opportunity to reach your own unique potential. Many of us are on a quest to "fit in" to an image or mould, but more often than not this takes us further away from our true selves. I'm a big believer that life will always take you back to where you need to be.

Becoming the best version of yourself requires taking responsibility for your thought processes, putting plans into action and feeding your soul. Every moment you're alive is a chance to live a profoundly fulfilled life, but to do so takes balance, reflection and intuition.

Achieving a balance of male and female energy in your life can be challenging. Most of us are dominated by one or the other— we're either more direct, looking forward in a straight line (the male/yang energy) or exposing our softer side and expanding the spiritual or metaphysical space around us (the female/ yin energy). When the pendulum swings too far one way, we run into trouble. Perhaps you're too caring and need to be more decisive and forthright, or too strategic to appreciate the human connections around you.

Another element of accountability is following things through and not giving up. Throwing in the towel is easy, but you'll never learn if you don't complete anything.

Even if it turns out to be a mistake, that's okay. You've still gained the knowledge of what not to do next time, and you've proven to yourself that you can see something through—that in itself is so powerful.

It's like the Cherokee parable about the dark wolf and the white wolf, two energies competing for dominance. When the children ask the medicine man which wolf will win, he replies "whichever you feed". Don't feed the dark wolf with self-doubt or fear. Clear out that bad energy and be accountable.

When it comes to making changes, don't try to take on too much at once. Pick up a little bit of information, bring in a new positive habit, then a few more, until it becomes easy to integrate it all together. And remember, your feelings are feedback, so listen to them and trust in them—they're trying to tell you something! Open up that line of communication with yourself, not just with others.

The wisdom to live your best life is already inside of you, you just need to find the courage to make it happen.

The real question is what are you going to do with it? For your business, your relationships, the planet—how can you harness what's inside of you, get some momentum and do something amazing?'

CHECKPOINT 3 WORKSHEETS

DEFINING YOUR VITAL INGREDIENTS™

01 PHYSICAL

Discussing a lesson as a class certainly boosts students' interest and engagement. Aside from helping them stay focused, it allows them to think deeply, create connections, and get different perspectives on the subject matter.

02 MENTAL

Discussing a lesson as a class certainly boosts students' interest and engagement. Aside from helping them stay focused, it allows them to think deeply, create connections, and get different perspectives on the subject matter.

03 EMOTIONAL/ SPIRITUAL

Discussing a lesson as a class certainly boosts students' interest and engagement. Aside from helping them stay focused, it allows them to think deeply, create connections, and get different perspectives on the subject matter.

NFM THE TRUTH MATRIX™

4 QUADRANTS OF COMMUNICATION

Honouring your truth & communicating without conflict ———

WHAT I THINK

HOW I FEEL

WHAT I WANT

WHAT I NEED

BLURTS

THIS RELATES TO: ————— — —————

RADICAL SELF BELIEF

"SUIT UP, LIFE HAS NO REMOTE, YOU MUST GET UP & CHANGE IT YOURSELF "

–Nikki

 RADICAL SELF BELIEF

4

CHECKPOINT
ACTION
TAKE THE LEAP
OF FAITH

RADICAL SELF BELIEF

action
/ˈakʃ(ə)n/

noun: action; plural noun: actions

the fact or process of doing something,
typically to achieve an aim

steps, measures, activity, movement,
work, working effort

The antidote to sitting in stress or failure, or feeling like you are not achieving anything, is to take action to do the next right thing and move towards happiness. This can be done even if you don't know exactly what that looks like.

If you have a vision for life and are connected to making your time here one of impact, you will know that there is only so much time you can run on autopilot before you need to do something different. More than ever, the world needs you to be courageous and progress. It needs you to step up, suit up and command a higher consciousness for your decision-making.

In Checkpoint 4, we put the ideas and revelations of what you want, need, think and feel into a more practical game plan to make the next right step. We'll go through this stage with the following pit stops:

- defining what your great looks like (THE WHAT),
- creating your 90-day plan (THE HOW), and
- finding and recognising your core pit crew—your inner circle of trust and expertise that will be part of shaping a successful journey (THE WHO).

The issue with the pandemic of overwhelm and overload is that, in today's society, we are often bombarded with all of the things we think we should be doing and achieving. This is the case without first taking the accountability required to ascertain if the goals, visions and things we are chasing are relevant or even resonate with our inner GPS.

Driver's Seat Rule #1: Be inspired by others, but run your own race and define what your own great looks like. Where will you take action?

Driver's Seat Rule #2: Back yourself. Anchor your goals into clear 90-day plans so that you can ensure they are relevant, they resonate and they can be achieved in real time. The last thing you want to do is set yourself up for failure by putting unreasonable expectations onto yourself and others.

Do not stay stuck by fear of failure or past programming. Choose curiosity as your GPS. Break free of all of that and pave your own way. By running through the 'engine' checks and planning in this checkpoint, you will start building a roadmap for yourself that is realistic, inspiring and gives you some milestones to achieve along the way.

DEFINING WHAT YOUR 'GREAT' LOOKS LIKE (THE WHAT)

We all grow up with a list of what we should be doing and achieving, and the expectations that were instilled in us as kids manifest in our ambitions as we get older.

We chase impressive titles or a prestigious place in society as we seek to reach the end of a race that doesn't really have a finish line. This is because once we've crossed one thing off our list, we move on to the next. It begins to define who we are, and our personal and professional lives fall out of balance.

The fact is, many leaders don't even think about defining themselves until after they've had a breakdown and lost the foundations they fought so hard to build. They might be able to tell you their job title or their bank balance, but they've never discovered their true sense of self.

How can you avoid this? Stop compartmentalising. Build and design a life and a career that reflects your identity and enhances your experience of yourself. Then the ride becomes a prize in itself. Once we work through our fears and recognise when we may be overwhelmed, we have the chance to change the script and the direction we are heading in.

This next step—Checkpoint 4: Action—requires us to take a leap of faith on that. It is moving out of the cycle of fear and discomfort into one of courage, vision and conviction.

What do I really want? What does happiness, healthy love, success, health and financial wellbeing mean to me? This does not refer to buzzwords but to the real feeling and actual achievements that would signify reaching those landmarks.

I like to refer to our truth as the chassis of a vehicle—it's the structure that all of the rest depends on. Strip everything else away and that is what is left. Ignore the quality of the foundation and the whole set up around it will crumble.

Ignore your truth of what you really want, what your inner GPS says is the right direction, and you will quickly become a victim of the outside world and less in charge of your own.

Use the below prompts to shift gears and have a look at where things were not going well (or are not going well) and define what your 'great' could actually look like.

As you do this, write out and acknowledge the blurts or negative comments that pop up as you dare to define your 'great'. This will reveal your subconscious programming and disempower that inner critic. Keep that inner critic, the blurts and the triggers out of your head and onto paper so that you are fully aware there is no subconscious sabotage. When you place limiting thoughts, that self-doubt and those judgements on paper (or even make notes in your phone as they pop up), those inner-critic comments lose their power.

Use the table below to dare to define what your great looks like. Be fearless and as specific as possible. Be as specific as down to $, time, energy levels, location, and anything else that may be relevant.

FINANCIAL		
From this	**To this—my great would be**	**Blurts (what comes up when I try to define what great would be like)**
Lack of cash flow		
Over-leveraged and borrowed over capacity		
Lack of knowledge or desire to have clear view of the current financials, personally and commercially		
Risking cash and making rash decisions		
Lack of transparency at home and at work		

Feeling fearful about finances and that there is no solution or no way out

Extreme stress and anxiety around financial future and consistency		

Inability to plan ahead with clear mind

Lack of communication with trusted parties over what needs to happen for productive advice		

Head in the sand

PROFESSIONAL		
From this	**To this—my great would be**	**Blurts (what comes up when I try to define what great would be like)**
Stagnant in career and productivity		
Lack of growth and vision/ideas		
Inability to make decisions or take initiative		

Loss of confidence
with peers, market,
industry and
customers

Loss of staff, clients
and opportunities

No enjoyment or
connection to the
why

Exhaustion and lack
of energy around
people, projects and
profit

Paranoia,
comparison and
feeling threatened

Perceived failure

Inability to lead

Avoiding decisions
or agility

Inability to
communicate clearly
and solve problems

Burnout

Lack of direction

'Head in hands' over
areas of concern and
stress

Want to 'give it all
away, throw it all
away, opt out'

PERSONAL		
From this	**To this—my great would be**	**Blurts (what comes up when I try to define what great would be like)**
Indecisive		
Confused		
Exhausted		
Disengaged		
Insomnia		
Numbing with alcohol, excessive TV, gaming, drugs; avoidance techniques		
Dysfunction and breakdown in friendships and relationships		
Lack of connection to others, including children, and to work		
Feeling out of control, unhinged and full of anxiety		
Lonely		
Disempowered		
Unfulfilled, lack of real intimacy and love without conditions		

"
LIFE IS NOT A DRESS REHEARSAL FOUNDATION, FOUNDATION, FOUNDATION
"

–Nikki

CREATING YOUR 90-DAY PLAN (THE HOW)

So, now that you've identified what great could look like for you and you have put the visible subconscious blurts down on paper, you know there will be a gap once you take action. How do you trust this space that occurs between leaping and landing?

You get to keep it simple and put a basic plan of action in place.

Any good strategy has a set of goals that are clearly visible and some core milestones laid out along the way. Think of this as your roadmap. There will be detours and roadblocks, but that's where the fun lies—in the uncertainty of life. Overall, however, you now know what you want to achieve and the core coordinates required to get to that destination.

Rallies are real. You need to be too.

Referencing the chart on personal and commercial shifts from chaos to celebration mode, where do you need to be in 90 days' time to turn these wishes into realities and firmly set your intent? What does that action plan look like for you?

- **90 days:** Are you clear on what facts and stats for achievements and results can actually be articulated and checked off as attained by the end of 90 days? For example, a savings plan, a friendship, a way to communicate, a specific project stage completed, or even a feeling in your own mental and physical wellbeing that you're on the right track.
- **30 days:** What actions would you need to take/see and be a part of in the next 30 days for the 90-day results to be achieved and in play?

- **7 days:** What immediate tasks, calls, activities, planning and information do you need to action over the next seven days for the wheels to be well into motion for your 90-day trajectory?
- **The now:** The three most crucial and easy-to-take next steps as of writing this list. The now.

Are your goals front and centre? And are you writing them down and taking notes as you navigate chaos to calm? Vividly describing your goals in writing is strongly associated with goal success. People who very vividly describe or picture their goals are anywhere from 1.2 to 1.4 times more likely to successfully accomplish them than people who don't. That's a pretty big difference in goal achievement, just from writing them on a piece of paper.[14]

When we actually write things down, we create a cognitive connection to our intent and our actions. This is a vital key in the neuroscience of performance and achievement. Part of the process, on a deep level, is called encoding.

Encoding is the biological process by which the things we perceive travel to our brain's hippocampus, where they are then analysed. From there, decisions are made about what gets stored in our long-term memory and, in turn, what gets discarded.

Writing improves that encoding process. In other words, when you write something down you have a much greater chance of remembering it.

---

14 Forbes.

So, when you are defining what your great looks like, and then making your 90-day plan, you are literally setting up coordinates in your brain that will determine the inherent direction you want to take.

To further cement our results and outcomes, we need to repeat this process at all stages. It's most important that we do this during the review and refine checkpoint, as it provides a cognitive connection to what we want and how we are going to get there.

At the end of this checkpoint you will find the 90-day plan worksheet for you to complete. It's also on the downloads in the online program portal. You need to do this four times a year. Driver, not autopilot. Set the coordinates before you embark.

Once you have this 90-day plan completed, do not bury it somewhere or hide it inside a file on your computer. Write it down, print it out and put it front and centre. Our results come from where we focus the most.

Don't skip steps*: Before you begin any of the next checkpoints, ensure you have anchored the core foundations correctly. This is recognising when you are out of alignment and being able to acknowledge your real needs, wants and desires without fear of reprimand. Keep checkpoints 1, 2 and 3 top of mind as you create your plans here.

YOUR PIT CREW

Your vibe attracts your tribe. You are the master of your destiny. Now you're moving yourself out of overwhelm and cluttered thinking to a much clearer runway. You're getting into the driver's seat.

Who do you need to communicate these elements to in order to ensure they are empowered to support you and understand the milestones along the way? KPIs in a work and personal sense— what actions would you need to have and see from others to best support your goals? How does that funnel down to your team and their support?

So, make sure you've got the best pit crew around you—a crew who actually wants to see you shine, to support you in the bad weather, to navigate the tough turns with you and to earnestly celebrate your success and happiness.

Who are you going to share this journey with? How do we amplify the wins, the grins, the lessons and the learnings? We find ourselves the very best pit crew, personally and commercially.

A great pit crew is an ecosystem. Your closest friends, your trusted family members—these are your fan club.

Then there's your technical team. This can comprise legal, financial planning—a great mortgage broker, for example, or an accountant—health and wellbeing advisors/coaches, professional and personal mentors, and so on.

It is essential to have this core group of friends and mentors who really challenge you and support you. We all need to have the ultimate support crew to call on whenever things get tough, but the flip side to this as a leader is learning the importance of reaching out to these people when the road is windy and the visibility low.

Personal or commercial, each relationship we have is vital to our overall sustainable success and happiness and our ability to really thrive in this crazy world of ours.

Be aware of dream stealers and energy thieves. Do a quick check on your traffic-light list in Survival Mode, and consider who around you pulls you down versus who adds value. You will know the answer straight away.

Who we hang out with and invest our time and energy into within our core inner circle and trusted sources is choice, not chance. A natural attrition will occur as you shift gently into a different gear of self-worth, value and vision.

- Allow this to unfold.
- Let go and release ties and people that no longer serve you. It may feel challenging, but that is the natural order of things. You have made a commitment to yourself in picking up this book that you are going to be engaged, on purpose and present in your own life.
- Don't rush to fill the voids.
- Allow room to have new people come in—don't replace just to fill the gap. Instead, understand the trigger this may raise for you, such as reflection or abandonment.

Bear in mind this journey you are taking is one of deep self-discovery. It's off the beaten track and there may not be the usual stops and hangouts. You will notice you need time to yourself to do the 'homework' on your basic wants and needs. This requires reflection and space from the ordinary freeway we used to take, day in and day out.

Always watch what people do, not what they say. It may be difficult to see this through at first, but as you raise your own focus to a more authentic place, the congruence of people around you will also improve.

Being challenged is different from being pulled down or experiencing the diminishment of your self-worth. Know your healthy boundaries upfront and share your vital ingredients with those closest to you so they can best understand what you need to feel well, balanced and at your personal best.

Things can be bought, but purpose, passion and people who truly understand and support you are priceless. So, choose wisely.

- Understand your capabilities and who you need around you.
- Surround yourself with people who are aligned not only with your goals, but also your personal values. Don't take shortcuts, as the people in your inner circle will need to be there for you in all conditions.
- Communicate clearly. Be accountable for your actions, needs and wants and be transparent. People are not mind readers. As you go through this process you and your needs will evolve, so please don't shy away from communicating with those closest to you during each stage.
- Nurture these relationships, just like you'd nurture a business connection—personal ones matter as well.

Collaboration, teamwork, mutual respect, empowerment, communication and honesty have real applications.

- What do you need from your team/family or friends to achieve your goals? Where can they best support you? Tell them.
- What do you need from your partner or closest friend to feel supported? Tell them.

All too often we 'pitch' a conversation at someone and then get annoyed when they don't show up for us. If you move out of ego and into a conscious grounded energy with clarity around your needs and wants, then all you need to do is stand by that truth and communicate with grace and transparency.

To do this, use The Truth Matrix™ (4 Quadrants of Conscious Communication) from Checkpoint 2 and the 'What your great looks like' column to anchor your conversations. It's also really helpful to share your 90-day plan with key stakeholders who are invested in you achieving your milestones and true destination. When you are creating your dream team (a.k.a. your pit crew) there are some tangible actions to take to ensure you have momentum and clear milestones to keep each other very accountable.

Be clear:
- Be direct.
- Ask for support in a clear, open manner; never assume people know what you need.
- Get informed to ensure you have the right questions for experts. Don't rush in until you have the facts and stats. Good advisors do not railroad or rush.
- Be curious.

As you get closer to leading at the top and defining your 'remarkable', you will find the genuine support around begins to diminish. This is not necessarily a bad thing. I believe that, at a certain point, having a small yet trusted set of sources, experts, friends and confidantes is better than having many. Quality not quantity. Let people's actions show their value—words are cheap and no reflection of another person's real ability to deliver on any level of friendship or otherwise.

Empower others to meet you in the middle, and bring their skills, hopes, dreams, ideas and energy to the table in their own way.

At the end of this checkpoint, you'll find a worksheet to help you recruit your pit crew.

As usual, before we move on to the worksheets for this chapter, let's hear from a leader who lives and breathes what I'm talking about here. This time I'm going to share the words of marketing juggernaut Chris Lochhead. According to Chris, it's all about habits that build up and create momentum. But he also knows that you need to breathe to course correct when you hit rough seas.

PIT STOP WITH CHRISTOPHER LOCHHEAD

'We live in a world obsessed with winning, but nobody ever talks about what happens after you win. What happens when you reach those goals and milestones you have been pursuing? What comes next?

A lot of senior executives and entrepreneurs face challenges when it comes to defining themselves. They might know they're a CEO or a CMO, but how does that translate to the rest of their life? When they step outside of their work role, who are they, really?

The most prevailing power you can have is who you are, not your title.

How do you interact with and treat others? Do you lead by example? Are you committed and smart? Can people count on you when it comes to the crunch?

When you're present and earn respect and admiration for your ideas and behaviour, you're accepted for who you are, not the positional power you have.

You may have been encouraged to think outside the box, but has anyone ever told you to look around it? We're not taught to look around corners, so we stay on this treadmill of school, uni, jobs, mortgage, house, kids, better job, bigger house... It takes a major crisis to force us to reflect on a better way of doing things, but this doesn't have to be the case!

There will always be peaks and troughs in your life, personal and professional successes and failures we need to face and overcome. The key is to be brave. Accept that it won't always be smooth sailing, and know that those blips on the radar are just that, blips you can bounce back from and become stronger, wiser, and kinder than before.

Every day we create and perpetuate the habits that inevitably propel us through life. It's all about momentum. Success doesn't rest on that one big decision or achievement that's changed your life. It's the ripple effect of all those little changes, those daily habits and intentions that have set you on this path.

You're the captain of your ship, and the direction you take is entirely up to you. You won't always have control of the landscape around you, but you can decide how best to navigate it.

When you get stuck, ask yourself what kind of problem this is. If it's a case of not knowing what to do, get some help or advice. But often you'll realise you do know what to do—it's actually putting that into motion that's holding you back.

Don't ask "what now?", ask "what if?" or "why not?" Don't just buy the book, download the podcast, or go to the conference, actually do the work, make the changes, take the leap. Look up, look around. Be curious and agile, ask questions.

You'll soon realise that the real reward is the journey. You get to have a life, a career, a business you've designed. There is no end goal, because you're living it every day.'

CHECKPOINT 4 WORKSHEETS

THE 90 DAY PLAN

PIT STOP

01 90 DAYS

What would you like to have achieved, feel like, actioned and cemented in terms of healthy productive habits in 90 days time.

02 30 DAYS

What actions, deliverables or things would be required in the next 30 days for those 90 day results to be a reality?

03 7 DAYS

What immediate actions need to be taken by you in the next 7 days. Where do you need to focus, source or what do you need to undertake in the next week to start the momentum.

04 3 IMMEDIATE

What 3 immediate tasks can you do as soon as you finish this list to go and start....think the most basic of actions. These are tangible elements - not goals.

ACTION MODE YOUR PIT CREW

01 CONFIDANT & CLOSEST ALLY

The one or two people who you can TRULY trust with anything. If you don't have that now don't worry as you embark on this journey you will find deeper friendships and connections that authentically resonate. Do not force this. You know straight away who to write down.

02 COMMERCIAL & PROFESSIONAL

Experienced, trusted sources around accounting, legal, professional, legacy, etc. Do a health check on who you have around you now and make sure you leave room to find the VERY best aligned support to advise you

03 PERSONAL & WELLBEING

Once again like the former category anyone you have advising you should have empathy, understanding, proven experience and be there to provide the best support and tools to suit YOUR goals. Not feed their own. A fun and crucial group - choose well.

04 EMOTIONAL/ SPIRITUAL

This is a tricky one as it really takes contemplation to ensure you are getting the right energetic, emotional and spiritual support. These people are wise, sound, grounded and practice what they preach. Choose wisely.

"LEADERS LEAN IN

—Nikki "

CHECKPOINT
REVIEW
AND REFINE
AGILITY VERSUS
RESILIENCE

review

/rɪˈvjuː/

noun

a formal assessment of something with the intention
of instituting change if necessary

synonyms: analysis, evaluation, assessment,
appraisal, examination

Since you are the driver in your life, like any top athlete, you need to be able to evolve as you set your sights high to enjoy the journey. I call this my Roger Federer Analogy.

When he's at the very top of his game, do you think that Roger Federer practises tennis and his mental aptitude elements more or less? The tennis balls do not come across the net any slower just because he has been number one for so long. In fact, there is more competition than ever before. So, this requires a continued application of the basic principles of his goals and his mental, physical and emotional wellbeing.

Mastering high performance means learning to refine, not reverse, and a winding road requires attention to detail and micro decisions. Let's pull over here to kick off Checkpoint 5: Review and Refine.

As Trevor Hendy said in Checkpoint 3: Accountability, 'the conditions are always perfect'. So, as you navigate through your world on a daily, weekly and monthly basis sustainable success comes from mastering the art of maintaining clarity and calm, regardless of the conditions.

Specifically, this is being on purpose and taking ownership on a regular basis, instead of just 'hoping for the best'. It is being consciously open to learning and refining.

In this checkpoint, we review the coordinates in place, identify and uncover roadblocks, and refine any actions or focus points by taking a moment to check our personal, financial, emotional and physical wellbeing milestones and behaviours.

In Checkpoint 5, we cover the following:
- Pit stops and the power of the pause—how to stop and assess where you are now versus where you are going.
- Lessons versus learnings—understanding and acknowledging what you need to prevent from happening again, and identifying which actions, behaviours and outcomes are working well and that you want to repeat.
- Review the 90-day plan and refine details on what you need to do next.

PIT STOPS AND THE POWER OF THE PAUSE

Do you recognise that feeling of starting a journey, in the car or whatever, and then arriving at your destination without any recollection of how you got there? It could be a simple trip to the grocery store or your daily commute to work. You arrived safely but didn't take any notice of what happened along the way.

In today's society, life has a certain pace to it. That pace is fast, and this means we need to review and refine our goals and needs much more often. We need to stay in touch with where we are going, rather than look up a year down the track and wonder why we got so far off course. You are your greatest asset, so why don't you review and refine your own roadmap as regularly as you would a business project?

Time is relative. Most people have long-term goals. They may be large scale, like setting up a business. They may be small scale but have a longer time frame to get there, like booking an overseas holiday or getting fit.

What used to take three to five years a decade ago now seems to unfold within a year—or a matter of months. Like any good rally driver or endurance athlete, we should be taking small but targeted moments to refuel. To ensure there is plenty of room to adjust and change course as required, without having to start all over again.

The problem with long-term goals that don't have small milestones to aim for along the way is that they often feel so distant it's hard to know where to start. So, it's hard to feel like you've achieved something and the payoff seems unreachable. Most goals and plans remain dreams; they get easily side-tracked because they're not chunked into bite-size pieces, like ninety days, for example. And they do not get regularly reviewed.

A term often used in a business setting to describe effective goal-setting is 'SMART'. Once an overarching plan has been established, such as 'increasing sales in product A', it's time to set small, achievable tasks for everyone. These goals are called 'SMART', which stands for:
- Specific
- Measurable
- Attainable
- Realistic
- Time-bound

We use SMART goals as the guide to organising lists and tasks that are directed towards achieving a desired outcome. They're checklists that are made up of small, actionable tasks that feel doable for the individuals and teams working on them—like our 90-day plan.

Smaller, regular reviews also prevent wasting time and resources on areas that are not in alignment. It is much easier to change direction from a pause position than it is to do it at full speed. Just like the teams that compete in motor sport at the highest level, such as Formula One or the Dakar Rally, you and your pit crew will get superefficient at these regularly scheduled opportunities to review and refine.

The same rules need to apply to our personal as well as our professional world. If you don't have a clear set of goals from your 90-day plan front and centre, then how will you know if you are on the right track?

How often should you press pause and do this?

As you start moving away from overwhelm and survival mode, I recommend doing the review and refine at the intervals noted below. This will ensure you are on purpose and will prevent you going back to the autopilot position that got you into overwhelm in the first place. The intervals are as follows.

a. **Daily:** 10 minutes—be on purpose, and set your intent at the start of each day.
b. **Weekly:** 15–20 minutes—ask am I on track; are the coordinates, activities and tasks I am applying myself to lining up? Sundays are a great day to do this so you can plan your Winning Weeks™.[15]
c. **Monthly:** Review and create your next 30-day plan, with reference to the current 90-day plan's desired outcomes.
d. **Quarterly:** Create the next 90-day plan, using the previous one as a reference point.

---

15 From my book FITPRENEUR Be the CEO of your Life as well as Your Business.

"THE CONDITIONS IN LIFE ARE ALWAYS PERFECT "

-Nikki

UNDERSTAND LESSONS VERSUS LEARNINGS

We seem to be constantly surprised by change and find ways to 'cope' with it rather than embrace it. It is vital to adopt a sense of agility, not just resilience. The result of doing the review and refinement of our goals more regularly, with clear focused intent, is that we can create a sense of agility (tiny clicks and shifts to realign with little effort) rather than resilience (having to bounce back after huge setbacks).

Every time you have the courage to press pause, you can also raise your awareness of what works and what does not. The key here is to separate the lessons (let's not repeat that) from the learnings (hey, that actually was pretty positive; maybe we can do more of this).

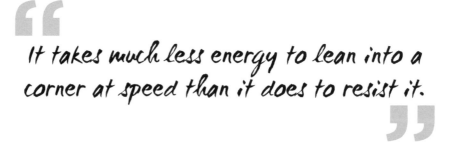

> It takes much less energy to lean into a corner at speed than it does to resist it.

Don't dwell on the hard knocks (the lessons). That would be to sit with the subconscious saboteurs: shame, blame, guilt and fear. Instead, use the hard knocks as a story or internal handbrake for the forward positive movement you have been creating. Own the setbacks, acknowledge them, but make sure you don't repeat them.

Learnings provide the extra energy and momentum that kicks in when you start to find your glide. To be efficient mentally we need to constantly declutter our 'hard-drive' space. What thoughts serve us and what do we need to release?

If you have a limited amount of storage space, you need to choose carefully which actions, people, behaviours and thought processes are going to come with you on your day-to-day journey.

Roadblocks come at all stages and all ages. They also occur more frequently the higher your level of performance. This may require mini check-ins throughout your day in the first few weeks as you raise your level of awareness around self (being grounded and conscious).

Don't avoid the triggers as they come up for your attention—just view them as a little bump in the road (not a total derailment) and quickly realign to the right path. All aspects of our life need to be considered for a sustainable journey. Do not leave any stone unturned.

For example, pay attention to the signs on the road:
- Relationship breakdowns and misunderstandings—are you experiencing small arguments, frustrations and not able to speak your truth clearly without conflict?
- Serious health issues or signs of ill health—are you feeling lacklustre, off colour and just ignoring the signs? Weight gain, weight loss, inability to focus?
- Neglecting the maintenance of your car, house or other elements that cost money and impact personal safety— have you ignored the basic maintenance and upkeep of the personal and professional aspects of your life and work that could end up costing you more down the track?

- Insomnia and anxiety—are you constantly feeling off-centre, over alert and on edge? Are you over thinking and unbalanced?
- Ignoring bills and important official documents—do you know you have personal and professional finances, taxes and aspects to deal with that you keep pushing out and don't want to look at for fear of what you will discover?
- Ignoring your own basic needs and wants—committing to the vital ingredients, but letting your day go by and not paying attention to those and then making excuses?
- Reacting rather than responding—allowing triggers, and other people's input and judgement steer you off course. Not using the four quadrants of communication to anchor your truth no matter what distractions are going on around you?

Ask yourself at this checkpoint: Are you applying the tools daily— journaling, setting intent and weekly planning?

Are you acknowledging the blurts and setbacks, then identifying the next best step, thought and action with a positive approach?

This checkpoint is when we do a regroup on our own ecosystem. We revisit the Traffic Light Worksheets: green (in flow), amber (stuck) and red (red flag, negative impact). The following tools from previous checkpoints can be deployed any time you feel you have encountered quicksand or bad weather:

- the Truth Matrix four quadrants (Accountability),
- the Traffic Light worksheet (Survival Mode), and
- the Ego and Blurts versus Wants and Needs worksheet (Awareness).

Remind yourself that tiny shifts in coordinates are more effective than having to double back and start again.

" A ROADMAP IS A FRAMEWORK, NOT A PRESCRIPTION "

–Nikki

REVIEW YOUR 90-DAY PLAN

At no point on this journey should you forget to check in with your 'log book': keep that 90-day plan front and centre.

Goals only work when we do. Pay attention to where you are putting your focus. These review and refinement moments allow us to stop and assess our previous 90-day plans. They allow us to see what, who or how we need to adjust our coordinates to match the landscape and be agile.

Revisit your intent.

Are all the items on your 90-day plan still relevant, exciting and important to you?

Review and refine what may need to be added and updated for the next 30-day segment and the next seven days, and what three tasks have to be actioned immediately.

Don't wing it; write down what you will bring forward and what you will leave behind by using the Lean In Worksheet at the end of this checkpoint. Ask yourself:

1. Are your overarching goals front and centre and keeping you focused?
2. Have you built time into your schedule to communicate with your pit crew—from accountability to stewardship?
3. Are you making the required 'me' time in your agenda for mindset and grounding?
4. Are you writing everything down and committed to your own dreams and goals?

Be deliberate.

Remove emotion and stories around things and think facts and stats. What do you need to be aware of? What do you need to be accountable for? And what are the next actions you need to take? Refer to the Lean In Worksheet.

> *It's not just our abilities and talent that bring us success but whether we approach them with a fixed or growth mindset.*
>
> -CAROL DWECK

Recalibrate. Remember, if overwhelm creeps in at any time and you start feeling anxious, stop and breathe for three minutes. That 180 seconds can make a difference to how your body reacts mentally and physically. I call this a quick and easy recalibration.

When we focus on our breath, it instantly brings us back to the present moment. Walk away from the phone, computer or situation just for a moment. Step away and go for a quick walk, have a glass of water, or just say 'I'll get back to you in five' if someone needs a response. Nothing is that urgent, unless it is a medical emergency. Remember, perspective is everything. Press pause and adjust your vision.

Be aware of the past but don't spend too much time looking back. There is a reason the rear-view mirror is smaller than the windscreen.

Whatever got you to this point, you're here; you survived.

Take a moment to remember that nothing in life is finite; you can adjust your sails as required or input a diversion on the roadmap if needed. Just avoid sudden drastic moves. Communicate clearly to yourself and to others from a place of calm and grace. There is always a solution. Happy review and refining, and welcome to really being in the driver's seat as you master the art of doing this regularly.

In this checkpoint, we're going to take a pit stop with Matt MacKelden, a high-performance driving instructor who has raced in a wide variety of events over the last decade and is a two-time class winner at the Bathurst 12 Hour.

He is a man who is not afraid of changing direction and re-drawing his roadmap when the conditions change. At the age of thirty he was dissatisfied and took a leap of faith that launched his racing career. But he wasn't above admitting that, years later, it was time to change direction again.

"THE ROAD OF ADULTING DOESN'T GET EASIER, WE JUST GET MORE AGILE. EMBRACE THE JOURNEY. "

-Nikki

RADICAL SELF BELIEF

PIT STOP WITH MATT MACKELDEN

'I'm forty-five years of age now and the last fifteen years have been really where I started to live my life. I reckon prior to that I was doing everything that everyone thought that I should do. Doing everything the social norms thought that I should do.

I felt relatively trapped and so I made a very brave decision, a decision I think a lot of people find very difficult and sometimes it's viewed as quite selfish. But I decided that this was my life and I needed to try and live it the best way possible. So, I ended up buying a race car—my first race car—when I was thirty years of age.

Having looked at racing my whole life and thinking, 'I reckon I could do that', I ended up taking some equity out of the house and bought my first little race car.

I couldn't even fit into the car, so had to lose weight. I gave up smoking instantly, going from a pack a day to nothing, lost thirty-five kilos, jumped into the race car for my first race, ended up qualifying fourth, coming second in the race.

All of a sudden, the new life of Matt MacKelden was underway. I was flying around the countryside, being in fabulous cars, meeting incredible people, and leaving my family at home.

After a while that gets very old. There's only fifty-two weeks a year and I did sixty-four flights one year. And that's a heck of a lot of travel. At the end of the day, yes, you earn good money and, yes, you have fabulous experiences.

But the reality was different. I'm happily married to a wonderful woman with two beautiful little girls, whose lives, you know, I wanna be a part of. To be a part of my step daughters' lives.

So, again, while it's all shiny and lovely on the outside, it is extremely hard work. It's also very dangerous work. One of the turning points for me was an event at Bathurst. After the Bathurst 12-Hour event, a customer in the driver's seat, while I was in the passenger seat, reached 287 Kilometres an hour down Conrad start.

I looked over and I knew immediately I had to get him to back off, but that flicked a switch within me and I thought, "Well these things are not getting any slower. I'm getting a little bit older here, and my wife and my family". I knew something had to change.

For the fifteen years I had been privileged enough and lucky enough to be able to make a living out of motor sport. In the sponsorship side of the business, driving as well, a commentator on Network 7 for a little while, calling the V8 super cars. I took control at thirty, and now at forty-five I've done it all again. I've gone from race cars to real estate and a nine-to-five job.

I was a little bit nervous about it, but certainly the motivations for it now are not just about myself. It's more now about my family.

Roadblocks exist when we make changes and usually these are from others' opinions. This is part of the journey—perhaps due to their own sadness, they will hate your success.

Even family, they will potentially try to hold you back, even if they're not doing it necessarily outwardly. I had the negative, "Matt, why would you go into real estate? It's a really bad market right now, and it's retracting, and why would you do this?" That's holding back. That's not support.

So, don't be afraid. Go easy on yourself. Give yourself a bit of a break, and then just be prepared to move and to act and to do the research, and just be careful about who you have around you.

Be polite, but don't invest all your time and your emotion in people who may be holding you back. They're holding you back because of their insecurities, not because of anything you're actually doing.

Will I be able to deal with getting up and going to an office every morning, with a desk and sales targets and expectations of all that kind of thing? Am I going to be able to deal with that, remembering that my office had been a racetrack for the last six or seven years?

Working nine months a year in the driver training field, with three months off every year, there were questions in my own mind as to how I was going to deal with that. There was even a concern for a little while there: How are we going to operate within our family unit with me being here all of the time? It's all a work in progress. But all of that was logistics; I had to make a game plan that meant I felt connected to my next decision, no matter what.'

CHECKPOINT 5 WORKSHEETS

THE LEAN IN WORKSHEET™

TAKING THE LEAP OF FAITH ON THE WHATS NEXT

AWARENESS

Identify the areas you feel you want to go, what is and isn't working and where that need to look around the corner at potential – don't ignore the little voice that says to you – "you need to try this, you can't NOT do it, just try, take one step, this ignites you".

BLURTS (WHY NOT)

ACCOUNTABILITY

Make a list of behaviours and elements you would need to put into practice to assist with healthy change and growth. What can you do for YOU (business or personal it's the same approach).

BLURTS (WHY NOT)

ACTION

How can you show up for yourself, what do you need to DO to actually create courage to lead in what you want. What specific steps to do you need to take next

BLURTS (WHY NOT)

THE TRAFFIC LIGHT WORKSHEET™

Drop the pin on what is in flow and where the biggest anxiety/stress and roadblocks sit. Be 100% honest. ——

GREEN (IN FLOW)   **AMBER (ON THE EDGE)**   **RED (OVERDRIVE/OVERLOAD)**

MENTAL
Where am I right now on this date - how am feeling,

EMOTIONAL
Where am I right now on this date - how am feeling,

PHYSICAL
Where am I right now on this date - how am feeling,

THE MOJO MAKER™   **RADICAL SELF BELIEF**

6

CHECKPOINT
CELEBRATE
AND REWARD
THE WINS AND GRINS

RADICAL SELF BELIEF

celebrate

cel·e·brate (sĕl′ə-brāt′)

verb: cel·e·brat·ed, cel·e·brat·ing, cel·e·brates

v.tr.

to observe (a day or event) with ceremonies
of respect, festivity, or rejoicing

"PEOPLE BELIEVE PATTERNS, NOT PROMISES "

When our mission resonates throughout all we do, it becomes a natural part of who we are. What do you have in place for recognising the daily rituals and habits that all add up to the larger result and reflect the vital ingredients and 'what great looks like'?

Creating ceremony cements positive habits and transforms results. Great sports teams do it; individual athletes do it; and legal institutions, schools, universities, religions, clubs and companies do it. Ceremonies exist everywhere.

In Checkpoint 6: Celebrate and Reward, it's time to define milestones so that we can keep up engagement and momentum. We also need to understand what type of rewards work best for you, and work out how you can engage and reward the people around you as well. We will look at the following.

1. **Ceremony and celebration**—why rituals are key to sustainable success.
2. **Identifying the milestones**—when and why you should celebrate.
3. **Setting and sharing the rewards**—Maseratis versus Marshmallows.

This is a short checkpoint, as most of the work needs to be done by you in the pit stop. Here are some guidelines to help set the scene and put your plans into action for the wins and grins.
Note your idea of rewards and ceremony will differ from others. Just make sure you take the time to identify what matters—remember, it's the simple things that really count.
When we value ourselves, we place less value on the things around us. Extra time, therefore, is often the most precious commodity of all.

CEREMONY AND CELEBRATION

Somewhere along the way, despite all the ways we have to stay connected, we have lost our daily rituals and our sense of gratitude—the ability to see how far we have really come.

What if this was it?

What if this was everything you were working towards, how you showed up for your day, the people in your life, the small wins, the milestones you are ticking off in flow one by one? What if you navigated change and challenges with a new sense of grace and self-belief using the grounded approach to press pause rather than panic.

How would that feel? How would you celebrate the small wins and the big grins?

Good health and wisdom require a strong connection to the world, to nature and to those around you. It is connecting the dots. This is the ceremony aspect we need to set up in our lives. When you take time out to celebrate and recognise how far you have come, it provides you with opportunities to unplug from this part of your life and reinvigorate your soul.

Setting goals is easy; achieving them is hard. Why? It requires you to put the work in to actually make it happen and be rewarded along the way. Never underestimate the power of celebrating what lies between the start and the finish line. Each stage, goal and milestone we set for ourselves is a valuable part of this journey.

A goal is any desired outcome that wouldn't otherwise happen without some kind of intervention. In other words, a goal is a detour from the path of least resistance.[16] So, when we are committed to making change and getting into the driver's seat, we cannot skip the neuroscience of celebration and reward for positive behaviour. This will ensure we stay motivated and on the right path.

According to research from Princeton University, when it comes to goal-setting, humans have two conflicting brain regions. One area is associated with our emotions and the other with abstract reasoning.

Short-term gratification (our emotion) often wins over long-term goals and abstract reasoning. This is due to the release of dopamine and what happens in our brains when we achieve a certain positive outcome.

Dopamine is connected to feelings of pleasure, learning and motivation. It's that positive energy, high-fiving endorphin that sends us a little bit giddy and happy—often from small amounts of success. Receiving small, regular rewards allows us to experience the effects of dopamine. Having experienced those effects, we become eager to repeat the actions that allowed us to reward ourselves in the first place—we want to get that dopamine hit again. Neuroscientists refer to this as 'self-directed learning'.[17]

---

16 Elliot T Berkman, the Neuroscience of Goal Setting.
17 Department of Psychology and Neuroscience, University of Colorado.

Therefore, we need to ensure we are celebrating and rewarding the right behaviour and milestones, not endorsing old patterns. The emotional part of our brain responds positively to instant gratification. When given the choice of cake now or broccoli later, this part of your brain pushes you to choose the cake.[18]

And then staying connected with others and having a shared accountability for goals stimulates creativity, performance and positive mental attitude.

The art of ceremony exists in the smallest of habits every day. It's making the bed in the morning, how we enjoy a cup of tea or coffee, looking out the window and giving a moment of thanks and intent before we start moving in our day. It's sitting down for Sunday brunch and not rushing; it's planning a special dinner to celebrate a small win or milestone—something as simple as seven days of setting intent. It's watering the garden and taking care of the things we own. It is the art of being present.

Have you created a sense of ceremony for how you show up for yourself?

How does your mission and goals translate to your day-to-day being, behaviours, how you set up your home, start the day, end the day, and so on?

Creating a sense of purpose and ceremony will amplify the small wins you make along the way and help you navigate through the challenges with real incentives that empower change and that are relevant and resonate with you.

---

18 Harvard University.

IDENTIFYING THE MILESTONES

The wins and grins worksheet is the point where we can look at what works well, what we have learned and what we need to leave behind. Overcoming challenges is also something to celebrate, so when you fill out that sheet, look at the lessons and learnings as milestones as well.

What are the small and regular milestone moments you can mark off on this current plan and what can you celebrate? Look at your 90-day plan and earmark some milestones. Plus, there are other examples as well where you celebrate the improvement of healthy habits, mindset and behaviours you want to reinforce:

- Doing your journaling every day on triggers as they arise is actually a pretty powerful tool to celebrate. It means you are mastering yourself over subconscious
- Celebrating a new team configuration in your business that works really well together.
- Meeting your daily fitness and movement goals.
- Having that truthful conversation with someone and showing up for yourself with integrity.
- Getting a new business deal signed off.
- Achieving your savings target—instead of blowing it all, take a predetermined amount and shout yourself dinner or go do something and take half a day just to play and have fun without an agenda.
- Hitting a turnover target at work/business or in terms of salary.
- Teaching yourself a new skill and finishing a certain level off, like learning the guitar, painting, or picking up a new sport you have always wanted to try.

At the end of this checkpoint you will see the worksheet for you to use your 90-day plan and assign some milestones, moments and timelines along the way, with some relative celebration and rewards that can give you the mental thumbs up that this journey is worth it. Reinforcing positive experience will override the past negative patterns if you keep it consistent and achievable.

"MARSHMALLOWS, NOT MASERATIS

-Nikki

"

SETTING UP AND SHARING THE REWARDS

Once you have listed the milestones you wish to celebrate and acknowledge on your 90-day plans and your goal sheets, the next step is to define how you want to celebrate—bearing in mind the healthy habits and centred rewards that amplify your positive new choices, not endorse old negative patterns.

> *Enjoy the journey (a.k.a. Gold stars for Adults™).*

In all my coaching, I encourage gold stars for adults. This means being fully aware of reaching and rewarding the critical milestones and ensuring each brick we build the future foundation on is solid and cemented before adding more.

How we celebrate and reward ourselves and those around us is vital. It is a moment that we can experience positive reinforcement and gratification—one of the very basic emotional needs.

Don't sabotage your goal itself by choosing a reward that is counterproductive—for example, eating healthy for seven days and then celebrating with a six-pack of donuts.

Really think about what will give you joy and a sense of achievement without counteracting the work you have put in.

A reward can be as simple as a gold star on a piece of paper on the fridge, as fancy as a dinner out with someone special, or it can be just giving yourself some time out for an hour and permission to go do something fun.

Rewards come in all shapes and sizes and for all types of activities that are significant to the individual.

When it comes to rewarding you and your pit crew, this is a great opportunity to set shared intent and mini milestones as well. That way we can always deliver and not over-promise. This builds trust and continuity. I always say to my clients marshmallows, not Maseratis, for more frequent wins and grins.

Whatever the goal is, you need to be willing to recognise the highs and the lows along the way and also look for small moments to celebrate success as well as the bigger ones.

What are some examples of good rewards and incentives?
- Savings/bonuses
- A weekend fishing/camping/surfing/golf activity with friends and/or family
- Time off work/being busy to detach and play—with no agenda for the day
- Dinner out or coffee/breakfast
- Breakfast or coffee out
- A night off watching a movie and not having to cook
- Spending time with loved ones without interruption
- Learning a hobby, sport or activity that you enjoy

- Trophies, certificates, small items to represent milestones
- A special meal, card or gift
- A visit to a place you love, like the beach, the mountains, or going off the beaten track and taking a mini break

Have you asked your peers and significant pit crew what would be the most fun elements to celebrate with you on a shared win or milestone?

Consistency beats the size of the prize. If you want to truly shift from chaos to calm, then the very simple, regular little wins that acknowledge elements from the weekly and monthly goals on your 90-day plans will be the way to go.

One of my favourite things to suggest when you're working towards significant milestones is to grab a favourite bottle of champagne or special bottle of wine (or something special along those lines), and write what the milestone is on the bottle in gold marker.

Then put the bottle away somewhere safe and open it when you reach the milestone. You could also replace a bottle of wine with anything from a coffee to a weekend away. You could frame a certain photo of building a house, your first office, making something from scratch—whatever is important on those milestones. You could put a voucher for dinner in an envelope, write the milestone on the outside, and put it aside until you have reached the goal.

Being respected and appreciated by significant others is one of the most fundamental human needs. People go to great pains to gain acceptance and approval from others; however, the most powerful relationship is the one we have with ourselves. Being under appreciated can cause resentment, shame, blame and guilt. Conversely, being appreciated is one of the most important factors that increases motivation and satisfaction, as well as health and wellbeing.

Are we rewarding and recognising our own work and how we show up?

Are we doing the same thing for those closest to us?

Happiness is amplified when it is shared.

Working with your pit crew enables you to network and collaborate. The added bonus at this checkpoint is, as you build your pit crew and dream team and set up the milestones, you can also cultivate shared wins, productivity and co-creation.

So, when you look at your team of experts and family, and you're setting your wins and grins and identifying core points in the journey, include them in your celebrations along the way.

As you take the time to look at your Wins and Grins Worksheet below, define the milestone moments and write down personal and pit crew rewards that are attainable and achievable.

Here's a short story from Play Bigger author and founder, Al Ramadan, on why ceremony, trips away and creativity are vital for enjoying this rally of life and leadership.

PIT STOP WITH AL RAMADAN

'Throughout my career, I've had the opportunity to be involved in creating things that don't even have a place in the market yet. I've been surrounded by innovative minds who are coming up with concepts that nobody even knows what to do with, and been a part of pioneering ideas that have fundamentally changed how everyday people think about and experience technology within their life.

My most recent role has been to take those who are already successful and established, and help them take their business to the next level and reach the ultimate transcendence through collaboration and consciousness.

But how do you take that leap from early adopter to creator or founder?

The key is to listen to yourself. Everyone can spot a problem; what most lack is the insight to solve it. If you already feel like you've identified a problem and have a creative idea for a solution, what are you waiting for? There's nothing stopping you from going after it.

Have trust in your crazy, out-of-the-box ideas and work on them until you make them happen. Some of the things we're so familiar with and take for granted today, like smartphones, the Internet and even frozen food, were all once just a crazy idea until someone made them happen.

Plug in to the community that has the power to make decisions and propel you forward—the influencers, investors and idea makers in your niche. Not everyone will buy what you're selling, but that's part and parcel of being an entrepreneur. Be prepared for critiques and knockbacks, and use them to improve your idea or tweak your strategy for your next pitch. Find your place within an ecosystem of like-minded innovators and founders so you can thrive.

And remember to think about what others need, not just what you want to sell. The fundamental element of success is recognising a key problem and creating a viable solution for it—a solution that those most affected will buy into. It might be a market problem or a technology problem, but whatever it is, you must think about how your solution will be received.

I call it the magic triangle—you need a great product design, great company design and great category design. You must know how you'll be positioned in the mind of the marketplace and understand the context within which your ideas will be received. Our brains need categories; they function as containers for us to sort information into. Innovators create new categories, not just new products within existing categories.

I also emphasise the need to step away and make the most of opportunities to recalibrate. For me, it's getting out into the great outdoors and hiking, sailing or surfing. You might prefer music, yoga, or reading. Whatever your title is, the important thing is that you switch off from your regular routine and regenerate. Turn your phone off, go "off the grid" and connect to a deeper wisdom within yourself. You'll be more in touch with your intuition, and this will lead you to make better decisions in business and in life.'

CHECKPOINT 6 WORKSHEETS

THE WINS & GRINS™

CELEBRATE & REWARD

WHAT DID WE LEARN

Write the big and small learning and lessons we need to be aware of and acknowledge.

WHAT WILL WE DISCERN

What areas, actions, people, actions and things need to not be repeated, considered before doing again. These are out of alignment and deplete energy and results

WHAT HAVE WE ACHIEVED

Write the big and small wins and things we are proud of.

WHAT WILL WE REPEAT

What areas, actions, people, actions and things need to be repeated as positive actions and habits that are in alignment and contribute energy

CELEBRATE AND REWARD
Ceremony and Celebration

REWARD/INCENTIVE

● ● ●   ● ● ●   ● ● ●

MILESTONE

RADICAL SELF BELIEF

" GETTING TO THE TOP IS ONE THING, STAYING THERE EFFORTLESSLY IS ANOTHER "

-Nikki

RADICAL SELF BELIEF

CHECKPOINT
SUSTAINABLE
SUCCESS
HOW DO YOU KNOW WHEN YOU'VE MADE IT?

7

RADICAL SELF BELIEF

sustainable

/səˈsteɪnəb(ə)l/

adjective

able to be maintained at a certain rate or level
able to be upheld or defended

Sustainable Success. What does that look like? It means to be fully in the rally of life. Regardless of what roadblocks and conditions are thrown your way, you back yourself. You trust your energy, the landscape and your pit crew, and you're always open to exploring what is around the corner.

In Checkpoint 7, it is helpful to remember that we are constantly evolving, and as you grow, your goals will evolve with you. Sustainable success requires a 'thrive mentality'. This is a mentality that understands that harsh lessons are just speed bumps and that learnings provide you with valuable insights and tweaks you can build upon and refine.

- Embrace the fact you are a pioneer
- Lead with clarity and conviction
- Amplify teamwork and collaboration.

Sustainable success is the ability to 'go to ground' at any given moment and sit in neutral before making drastic decisions. It's having the right fuel and resources.

It's that spark you feel when you have a clear vision. That may change several times throughout the journey, but you know that no matter what others may say, you have the remote. You are in the driver's seat.

YOU ARE THE PIONEER

Great leaders never stop learning.

Not only do they constantly seek out new knowledge and experiences, they also put them into practice and embed these new skills into their lives. In this book, I wanted to remind you why you are a leader, regardless of your title. To remind you of your role in life as a pioneer.

There are certain attributes that reflect your ability to show up for yourself and for others as you navigate through personal and professional landscapes. They help you change family history and old patterns if needed, and create a new pathway for you and future generations.

These attributes include:
- being accountable;
- having a clear vision;
- championing change;
- communicating;
- developing others;
- collaborating;
- setting stretch goals;
- innovating;
- making time;
- being a role model;
- making an emotional connection; and
- creating sustainable and achievable promises to yourself, your team and family.

LEAD CLARITY AND CONVICTION

As you read this, resist the urge to overcomplicate your goals, achievements and rewards. Remember what you truly want to achieve for now. What tools, resources, people and places are the required mix to get you there?

If you overcomplicate, you will invariably end up with more wires to untangle, which prevents a glide through change (a.k.a. paralysis by analysis).

Part of working on goals and aligning with your inner circle (pit crew) is ensuring you are clear on how you can create connection and collaboration, and bring out the best in yourself and those around you in the process.

Use this checkpoint to ensure you're dropping the marker again and have clarity on your why, what and how. It is an annual mission statement for your entire life—not just work, but the total you.

(What) MY MISSION IS:

Is your mission clearly stated on a macro level as a whole statement?	Can you articulate this to others with conviction and clarity?	Do they know how they fit into that picture and what you need from them as your pit crew?

(Why) VISION—THE REASON BEHIND ALL OF THIS IS:

Do you really know and back your WHY? What is your personal drive behind your goals and mission?	Can you articulate this WHY to others with conviction and clarity?	Do they know how to amplify that for you and repeat that without your founding WHY getting lost in translation?

(How) VALUES: WHAT ARE YOUR NON-NEGOTIABLES TO SHOW UP FOR YOURSELF:

Have you set your vital ingredients up, plus outlined what you do not want? Are they on paper?	Can you articulate how these values are demonstrated (in other words, the behaviours that reflect these important elements)?	Do your pit crew and those in your closest ecosystem understand the values you honour and how they reflect in all you do, are and say? Are there examples of how to demonstrate the best version of these during change, and manage expectations?

TEAMWORK AND COLLABORATION

I firmly believe that companies today are our new communities. I personally believe that we need more support for dynamic, true, values-based leaders running businesses, driving communities, and teaching families and teams to find that absolute blend of enjoyment, good values and financial success, and to share in all of the abundance that can be created from sustainable results. By doing so, we can create a ripple effect of positive, healthy, strongly-led cultures.

When we work to truly empower leaders, we create a ripple effect. That effect flows through organisations, colleagues, families, children, schools and, ultimately, our interaction and values between ourselves and one another.

Whether you are a sole proprietor, a small business or a large multinational, your culture is the by-product of your values and behaviour. By working on culture with leaders and companies, we are in turn creating cultures at home.

As a leader, ensure you create an energy and a culture that thrives with passion and purpose, as well as conversations that create a real sense of connection. To do this, you must embody these things in your own life. These cannot just be words on walls. This must be done by the actions we take as leaders when we hit roadblocks and failures as much as when we achieve big wins and shared success—it all counts.

I often find a common thread in the upbringing and early life of great leaders. While they may differ from time to time, the leaders I know always have an undeniable work ethic that is powered by their self-discipline and self-belief—a sense of courage and the ability to enjoy the roller coaster we call life.

As a leader, it's your responsibility to build trust, and the best way to do that is by being authentic. High performance and KPIs are important, but it's kindness and integrity that sets great leaders apart. Good leaders instil empowerment and engagement in their organisation; they lead by example and bring intellect to all that they do.

"

A SENSE OF PURPOSE IS A PRIVILEGE

"

-Billie Jean King

You're not only leading others, you're also raising the future generation of leaders. You might think you're driving the culture of a company, when in fact you're a leader in life, creating a knock-on effect in the lives of your employees, their families and the community, and influencing their mindset and approach.

That culture starts at the top and filters down. So, when you're a leader who collaborates, supports and communicates, that's the culture you'll be fostering in your organisation. Good culture creates a sense of community, and that's when you're able to develop a shared intent.

Remember, good communication is not confrontation.

It is crucial that those closest to you know what the frameworks for review are and how to communicate.
- Never assume everyone else thinks the way you do
- Always ask questions
- Agree upfront the wins and milestones to be celebrated

Loop back and acknowledge what isn't working, and then be specific about it to facilitate growth or a change in approach. This fosters confidence, unity, community and accountability. It fosters teamwork and, most importantly, significance. Review the goals and checkpoints regularly as you grow; the market changes, we change and the parameters we work off need to be adjusted accordingly.

This all applies at work and at home. Personal relationships and commercial relationships should be built on a solid foundation but also one of genuine connection.

When you're authentic and accountable, your leadership will be celebrated and you'll get people to buy in from the start. It's not just about profit, it's about people and purpose too.

Before we get to this pit stop for this checkpoint, I'll mention the final worksheet that follows it: The Fun Factor. So many of us forget to play. Fun, joy, energy and happiness are the most priceless rewards of all. What will make those your new normal?

Take a moment to put your ideas down on paper. What lights you up? What do you love to do and would love to do—the accessible and the bucket-list worthy?

If you don't define what you want, you'll get what you're given. The ability to be a great leader isn't defined by a job title. It's not given or earned. It's a verb—something you do each and every day.

Now, to leave us with some thoughts for sustainable success and leadership, we will loop back to some words from James Hunter, Managing Partner, KPMG.

PIT STOP WITH JAMES HUNTER

'Leadership is constantly evolving, but at its heart, good leadership is authentic. You can't read a book and decide to be like someone else; you have to have your own style and be true to yourself. Many of us are born with the traits and skills that make a good leader, but most don't utilise these effectively because they haven't been mentored or supported through life.

You can't be a successful leader without trusting those around you. When you're accountable on a global or regional scale, you simply cannot do it all yourself. Certainly, when you put your trust in others, you'll look at their track record of delivering results, but the integrity of their character and a shared alignment are just as important.

When you share a vision of what a great result will look like, people feel so much more integrated and we as leaders are able to learn from them, rather than merely having them comply with us. We can set that vision, create an understanding of what needs to be done and why, and trust our colleagues to deliver. It's a delicate balance between empowering them to tackle what's required of them and trusting their capability, while also making yourself available should they need to clarify or seek advice.

They may be reluctant to ask for help, so ask them "How can I support you?", then pause to let them respond. Make it clear that it is a place without judgement, that you want to understand them and their needs and get to the root of the issue.

Today's companies are a diverse melting pot of backgrounds and expertise, and this can play a part in the evolution of culture. To ensure the culture doesn't become diluted or deteriorate, you need to be a good communicator. Don't rely on structures or hierarchies. Adopt a flat organisation matrix that allows people to experience first-hand your authentic leadership and then replicate it in their own interactions with others.

Value statements are often plastered on walls throughout organisations, but this means nothing. Values aren't something you can put on a poster; they are defined by the things you do and say each day, the way you conduct yourself in work and in life. If there are people in your organisation who don't live these values, letting them go regardless of their results or sales sends a powerful message that these values are non-negotiable.

You don't need copious policy and procedure manuals or rule books to drive good culture. Instead, promote those values from the very first day you induct new people into your team. Show them how they too can be good leaders and make a difference, through mentoring and coaching. Remember, people don't work for you; they work with you to deliver outcomes.'

"YOU WILL NEVER HAVE MORE TIME THAN YOU DO RIGHT NOW "

-Nikki

RADICAL SELF BELIEF

CHECKPOINT 7 WORKSHEETS

THE FUN FACTOR

The crucial what's this all for if you can't enjoy the journey – Pit Stop

LEVEL 1: ABSOLUTE WOULD LOVE LOVE LOVE TO DO THIS...

And could probably do this very easily - just have to get off my butt to do it. Been meaning to do this actually......

BLURTS

LEVEL 11: THIS WOULD BE SO COOL TO DO AND I HAVE BEEN THINKING ABOUT IT FOR EVER LEVEL 11

Would take a bit more logistics, $ etc but still totally on the list

BLURTS

IF I COULD DO ANYTHING AND NO ONE/NOTHING COULD STOP ME - ANYTHING WAS POSSIBLE LIST - THE DREAM LIST LEVEL 111

If nothing or no money was an object this is the list of REAL DREAM makers of a life time for me.....

BLURTS

PURPOSE, VISION, TRUST AND COURAGE

-Nikki

THE AFTER PARTY

RADICAL SELF BELIEF

Following through on your destiny. Dare to pioneer.

The following are the 10 Commandments of Adulting the Rally of Life.

1. Trust your silly ideas.
2. Ask for help if you need it, and have good people around you.
3. Be curious, not fearful.
4. Own your stuff and learn from it.
5. Have empathy for yourself as well as others.
6. Don't be a victim; it's not sexy or productive.
7. Cultivate your consciousness—no autopilot, listen to your heart, keep evolving—it's pretty cool.
8. Concentrate on your own actions instead of trying to control others.
9. Lead by example. Everyone needs a beacon of inspiration, authenticity and courage—if you've got it, then lean in.
10. Never judge others—life is by choice, not chance.

" LIFE IS LIKE A BICYCLE: THE ONLY WAY TO TRULY FIND BALANCE IS TO KEEP MOVING "

-Einstein

What will you do to change the way the world works? Before you answer that, first ask what will you do to change the way you work?

To truly adult the rally of life, we must lead by example. Replace fea r and inertia with curiosity and action. Create momentum, forward movement and empowerment through increased awareness of your individual purpose, education and personal development. Share those learnings and your vision with a sense of collectivism and collaboration.

The only challenge I put to you is how can you 'suit up' and 'show up' for yourself? We all know what the right thing to do is, but true courage is to release the fear of perceived conflict and failure and back yourself.

I dare you to pioneer; to stand tall; to trust your crazy ideas; and to raise the bar and support equality, individualism, personality and purpose.

As you know now from reading through this book and doing the worksheets, being in the driver's seat requires focus and determination.

You know that sustainable success is a fine blend of commercial success, physical sustainability, emotional maturity and mental clarity. It is the notion that, if you lead with your physical, emotional and mental toolbox (checkpoints 1 to 4), you will harness that ultimate consciousness.

This is empowering you to recognise signs when things are getting out of alignment and shift your coordinates ever so slightly so that you stay true to your own path.

- You know when to recognise the signs you are getting triggered and overwhelmed, so you press pause and become accountable for shifting gears and not pushing yourself.
- From here, you know your vital ingredients and what lights you up, how you best operate and where the moments of happiness are most easily ignited and found.
- You have the aptitude to set a roadmap for your goals and break this down into bite-size, achievable milestones that ensure achievement and wins along the way. Your ability to clearly communicate what you think, feel, need and want empowers you to stay connected to your vision and also empowers others around you to support and co-create.

Finally, at any given point, you press pause and review and refine the now so that you understand the importance of micro shifts to ensure effective energy, flow and momentum in all you do.

From here, you know you can trust a solid foundation.

You are ready to go: suited up with a fresh perspective that this is a journey of progress and not perfection, showing up with a new set of road rules, grounded in your truth and elevated by the vital ingredients for energy, drive and conviction.

Supported by an excellent pit crew, celebrate the mini and the big wins, the falls and the recovery, all underpinned by an almost dogmatic approach to rest, rejuvenation, review and refinement along the way.

The fact is, no one can stop you from being your personal best and setting a positive example by putting the work in to achieve what you want most in this world. You are the creator of your destiny.

Do not wait to make an impact. Do not walk past a moment where you can create significance for someone. Be mindful of your words, your energetic vibration—your deep intent.

Be fearless; don't be afraid. Don't be scared to make a decision, to follow through and follow your heart. Encourage your kids to do so, too.

And lastly, be aware of your thoughts, of your truth. We can be so hard on ourselves. We are so programmed that by twenty-one we've got to have a degree, by twenty-five we've got to look like 'this', we've got to be married by thirty, and then we've got to live in a big house. It's time to write your own script. Keep going back and refining as you evolve along the way.

Oxygen mask first: You've got to be happy and on purpose first and foremost, a contributor to society rather than a follower.

Be ready. Suit up. Preparation is the key. If you want something, work for it, prepare for it. Be adventurous.

Take the road less travelled and trust your inner GPS—it knows the way.

Nikki

FINISH LINE

RADICAL SELF BELIEF

"THERE IS NO GREATER REWARD IN LIFE THAN REALISING THIS JOURNEY IS ONE OF INFINITE POSSIBILITIES "

—Nikki

RADICAL SELF BELIEF

GUEST INTERVIEW BIOGRAPHIES

JAKE EDWARDS

After experiencing his own struggles with mental health and addiction, former AFL footballer Jake Edwards was determined to make a difference in this under-resourced area. He founded the successful Australia-wide welfare and education organisation Outside the Locker Room, dedicated to working alongside local sporting clubs to offer mentoring support and education on topics such as drugs, alcohol, depression and suicide.

Today, Outside the Locker Room supports more than 3,000 young adults and their families, and Jake has established himself as a prominent voice in mental health advocacy, thanks to his passion, education and innovative approach.

Jake is an accomplished public speaker, and has been invited to share his experiences and Outside the Locker Room at functions for lululemon, F45, EML, Adelaide University School of Law and AFL Victoria. He has visited more than eighty secondary colleges and has been featured on SEN, Triple M, Studio 10, The Daily Show, Fox Footy, ESPN and Channel 9. He has also worked with leading organisations including Lifeline, Beyond Blue and the AFLPA.

Listen to the podcast with Jake.
https://thevitalitycoach.com.au/tmm099-jake-edwards-bro-code/

ANDREA MARCUM

Los Angeles-based yogi Andrea Marcum has a unique ease and familiarity about her. Weaving accessible philosophy into the poses, Andrea loves guiding the most unassuming newbies to yoga and mindfulness and works with athletes such as Matt Kemp of the LA Dodgers, global brands such as lululemon, Equinox, NBCUniversal, celebrities, and everyone in between. Andrea believes our yoga mats are magic carpets for looking into our lives and seeing the world, and she leads workshops and retreats around the globe.

Her critically acclaimed book, Close to Om, was described by Publishers Weekly as 'an inspiring guide for both beginners and seasoned practitioners' and is available from St Martin's Press/ Macmillan in hard copy and as an audiobook, which is read by Andrea herself. Andrea teaches at Yogaworks in LA, and you can practise with her from anywhere in the world on the Udaya and Gaia online platforms.

Listen to the podcast with Andrea.
https://youtu.be/zCq-GJytNcY

TREVOR HENDY

Trevor Hendy is one of Australia's most successful Ironmen, a six-time winner of the Australian Championship and four-time champion of the Uncle Toby's Super Series. Trevor is a member of the Australian, Queensland, Gold Coast and Surf Lifesaving Halls of Fame, and was inducted into the Sports Australia Hall of Fame in 2000, winning an Australian Sports Medal in the same year. In 1996, Trevor was made a Member of the Order of Australia for his services to surf lifesaving.

Later in his career, Trevor switched to kayak paddling and made the Australian kayaking team in 1998 for the World Championships and World Cup season. After a successful European summer, in which he medalled as a part of Australia's K41000m combination, Trevor returned home and announced his retirement. Although he no longer trained or competed in a professional capacity, Trevor continued to win Australian Championships into the early 2000s.

Since retiring from sport, Trevor has forged a career as a motivational speaker, life coach, mentor and author, and regularly appears on television and radio. His motto, 'the conditions are always perfect', has inspired countless others to pursue their dreams, regardless of the challenges they face along the way.

In 2012, Trevor launched his own website as a place to share his story and wisdom with others.

Listen to the podcast with Trevor.
https://thevitalitycoach.com.au/episode004/

CHRISTOPHER LOCHHEAD

Christopher Lochhead has been an advisor to over fifty venture-backed start-ups, is a venture capital limited partner and a former three-time Silicon Valley public company CMO and entrepreneur. He is also the co-author of two bestsellers, Niche Down and Play Bigger.

He has been called 'one of the best minds in marketing' by The Marketing Journal, a 'Human Exclamation Point' by Fast Company, a 'quasar' by NBA legend Bill Walton and 'off-putting to some' by The Economist.

Christopher served as a chief marketing officer of software juggernaut Mercury Interactive, which was acquired by Hewlett Packard in 2006 for $4.5 billion. He also co-founded the marketing consulting firm LOCHHEAD, was the founding CMO of Internet consulting firm Scient, and served as head of marketing at the CRM software firm Vantive.

Christopher is a dyslexic paperboy from Montreal with Scottish roots. After getting thrown out of school, with few other options Christopher started his first company at the age of eighteen. After over thirty years in business he has earned a PhD from the school of hard knocks, experienced the bliss of winning, the pain of failure, and learned how to laugh about the whole thing.

He loves family and friends, thinks the Ramones are legendary, believes George Carlin was right and loves riding the mountains and waves of Northern California.

Listen to the podcast with Chris.
https://thevitalitycoach.com.au/tvc082-life-after-awesome-chris-lochhead/

MATTHEW MACKELDEN

Professional driver trainer Matthew Mackelden has raced in a wide variety of events over the last decade, but is locked into a full SuperUtes season aboard the Kubota Racing Toyota Hilux in 2018. From racing cars at Bathurst, to finding buyers their dream homes in real estate, no one is more 'driven' than Matt.

Matt has enjoyed living on the Gold Coast with his family for over 20 years—and he loves it. Yet he has experienced his own journey in moving through challenges in life and understanding the importance of self worth, valuing family, health, wellbeing and the importance of a direct and positive mindset.

Mackelden has raced everything from Formula Vees and Hyundai Excels to Production Sports Cars, and is a two-time class winner at the Bathurst 12 Hour.

National categories in which Mackelden has competed include the Mini Challenge and Australian Production Car Series.

He has also been a familiar voice at Supercars events, filling the role of on-track commentator for categories including Australian GT Championship and V8 Utes.

Listen to the podcast with Matt.
https://thevitalitycoach.com.au/tmm095-matt-mackelden-in-the-drivers-seat/

AL RAMADAN

Al Ramadan designs categories for a living. In his own words, he is 'on a mission to create the next generation of enduring companies'.

Al started his career as a mathematician and software engineer—an old school data scientist. He cut his teeth writing Fortran 77 on a VAX 11/780 and still writes the odd piece of Python code. In the 1980s, Al built real-time analytics engines for big steel manufacturers and brewing companies.

In the early 1990s, Al applied data science to the America's Cup, creating a new category of sports performance analytics. Later he applied this vision to the Internet, creating a new category of digital sports media. His company, Quokka Sports, revolutionised the way people experience sport. The Quokka legacy runs deep in most sports coverage we experience today.

Al then joined Macromedia and Adobe, where he spent almost ten years changing the way people think about the business impact of great digital experiences and mobile. He led teams creating the Rich Internet Applications category and a new generation of mobile products and services.

After more than twenty years as an operating guy, Al turned his attention to being a legendary coach for entrepreneurs and teams wanting to change the world. He was named one of the most influential people in the digital economy by Time magazine, his research has appeared in Harvard Business Review, he has taken companies public and he is a co-author of the bestselling book Play Bigger.

Al loves the outdoors and remote expeditions. He has hiked the John Muir Trail, sailed in the Sydney Hobart Yacht Race, surfed Mavericks, lived on remote atolls in the Pacific and Indian oceans, and can often be found bombing back-country lines around Tahoe on a split board.

He is also a mentor, father and favourite uncle to the next generation, and has an uncanny knack of bringing out the best in kids, teenagers and young adults.

Listen to the podcast with Al.
https://thevitalitycoach.com.au/tvc068-play-bigger-al-ramadan/

JAMES HUNTER

James Hunter is an Australian KPMG partner with corporate experience across defence, education, construction, industrial markets, energy and utilities, and fifteen years in a diverse range of leadership roles in professional services in Australia, regionally and globally.

James' focus over the last decade has been working closely with companies across all sectors to deliver large, complex transformation and customer, digital and cultural reform programs in Australia, North America, the UK, Europe and across Southeast and Northern Asia.

In July 2013, James joined KPMG's National Executive Team as National Managing Partner, Markets and Growth, and is part of the KPMG Global Markets Executive. In this role, James has responsibility for all eighteen sectors, Australian accounts, alliance partners and the major client programs. James works with KPMG's global leadership, global and national lead partners, sector leaders, and divisional and alliance leaders to help leading audit, assurance and risk, deals tax and legal, management consulting and enterprise businesses provide the best client outcomes and create clients for life.

James has overall responsibility for KPMG's clients and markets, its strategic growth, and the firm's Asian and international corridors.

Listen to the podcast with James.
https://thevitalitycoach.com.au/tmm103-james-hunter-leadership-mojo/

ABOUT THE AUTHOR

Nikki Fogden-Moore, known as The Mojo Maker©, specialises in Quantum Coaching for the world's best leaders. She works with CEOs, entrepreneurs and high achievers on what's next to create value-led commercial and personal success.

The ultimate high-performance expert, Nikki's decades of experience lie in truly blending both commercial and personal acuity. Described as a rockstar in her field, she is innovative and passionate, has a unique ability to thrive in challenging environments, and is renowned for practising what she preaches. Nikki engages in next-level thinking to create harmony and purpose. Using her business and wellbeing expertise, combined with a proven set of highly accurate intuitive skills, has made her a remarkable coach and asset to her clients in and out of the boardroom.

Her models, such as Winning Weeks©, The Truth Matrix™, QDM™ Series and The Vitality Bank™, are proven tools for both teams and individuals in leadership.

Nikki is engaging, empowering and authentic in her experience and commitment to her work and clients. Author of *Vitality, Fitpreneur, The Wake Up Workout™* and creator of The Quantum Decision Making Program™ for extraordinary leaders, she divides her time between private coaching, Corporate Vitality,

Boardroom Retreats©, and writing and hosting her podcast, *The Mojo Maker.*

Working with Nikki, you will find an extraordinary coach and navigator who excels in showing the blueprint for what is next and remarkable, and for bringing fresh ideas to the table that are relevant and sustainable.

As well as having a Bachelor of Commerce and over a decade's experience in advertising and global brand strategy, Nikki was head trainer for Women's Health & Fitness magazine. She is a regular contributor to and often featured in business and lifestyle publications such as the *Huffington Post, CEO Magazine, the Sydney Morning Herald, Body and Soul, BRW, The Australian, Channel 7, Women's Health, Men's Health, Inside HR, NETT Magazine, The Daily Telegraph, Women's Health & Fitness, New Idea and Australian Financial Review.*

Connect with Nikki on

Linkedin/nfogdenmoore

Instagram/nfogdenmoore and Facebook/nfogdenmoore

nikkifogdenmoore.com or thevitalitycoach.com.au

Subscribe Youtube/VitalityCoachTV and podcast The Mojo Maker on Spotify and iTunes

REFERENCE LINKS

https://www.princeton.edu/pr/news/04/q4/1014-brain.htm

https://www.inc.com/sonia-thompson/want-to-grow-your-business-exponentially-stop-focusing-on-instant-gratification.html

https://www.ncbi.nlm.nih.gov/pmc/articles/PMC5854216/

https://grey.colorado.edu/mediawiki/sites/mingus/images/c/c0/HerdMingusOReilly10.pdf

https://www.forbes.com/sites/markmurphy/2018/04/15/neuroscience-explains-why-you-need-to-write-down-your-goals-if-you-actually-want-to-achieve-them/#16b7fb4a7905

Lightning Source UK Ltd.
Milton Keynes UK
UKHW051114230622
404851UK00006B/124